❋ *Bonnie's Household Organizer*

Bonnie's Household Organizer

The Essential Guide for Getting Control of Your Home

Bonnie Runyan McCullough

Illustrations by Tom Smith

ST. MARTIN'S PRESS · New York

*Dedicated to those who seek
the rewards of order . . .*

Acknowledgments
Special thanks to the many people who have given
help and support:
 Barbara Anderson, my editor at St. Martin's Press;
and Glenna Berg, my editor at home; to my husband
and children for carrying part of my load; to my
students for listening and sharing; and to the following
good friends—Sharon Causey, Ruth Hansen, Bryce
Jackman, Marilyn Jensen, Debbie Kelly, Arlo Luke,
Duane Peterson, John Pratt, Margaret Talbot, Nancy
Taylor, and DeAnna Troxell.
 Ensign Magazine has given permission to print
information from an article, "Teaching Responsibility
to Young Children," written by me.

Library of Congress Cataloging in Publication Data

McCullough, Bonnie Runyan.
 Bonnie's Household organizer.

 1. Home economics. I. Title. II. Title: House-
hold organizer.
TX147.M28   640   79-25525
ISBN 0-312-08791-8

Contents

Five * Taste, Nutrition, and Money

Six * Problem Solving

Introduction

Is your home sometimes out of control? Would you like to get organized? Do you ever feel like a slave in your own home? You can be the master. You can get control—by making the principles of good time management and organization work for you.

I am neither a born organizer nor a wonder woman with boundless energies. It has been a battle all the way, but you can learn from my experiences. Even though I began studying home economics in college, I gave it up to go into private practice. At first I was frustrated and felt stifled at home caring for babies (I've changed 5,478 diapers and washed 193,452 dishes). But I made the decision to become a professional home manager, not just a common laborer. In my quest, I have taken successful business principles and applied them to the home. These have been refined, broadened, and clarified in eight years of teaching home organization.

Everywhere I turn, I hear people say, "We just can't get organized at home." In a survey that I took of 125 families, it was shown that 91 percent had serious homemaking problems in at least one area. I have written this primarily as a source book of the principles and secrets of getting control of your home. Although most home care is done by women, these techniques apply to students, husbands, singles—to anyone tackling the job. And they can be applied to nearly every size, type, and style of home. It doesn't matter whether you live in a one-room apartment or a ranch-style house, or whether you are nineteen or forty, or whether you prefer Victorian antiques or pillows on the floor; you'll save time and money by following the concepts of organization, storage, maintenance, shopping, and problem solving outlined in this book.

Because not every home or home manager has the same problems, I've divided the book into many short chapters so that you can quickly find the exact information you need. If your home is awash with clutter and you need immediate help, turn now to Chapter 5 on minimum maintenance (MM). My students find that the MM technique instantly improves their homes and restores their sanity. (It was the MM technique which enabled me to put my house on hold while I wrote this book.)

My aim has been to fill this book with as much practical and helpful advice as possible. If you feel that you're spending too much time cleaning your home and trying to get organized, the suggestions in this book could help you get better mileage by accomplishing twice as much with half the effort. It will help you decide what you want your home to be and how much time you want to spend keeping it clean. It will show you how to create more free time by taking a few minutes each day to plan ahead for meals, shopping, appointments, and work. There are many ways to invest time now, which will pay off in dividends of more time later on.

If you have a roommate, you'll find suggestions for dividing the work without creating hostilities. If you have children, you'll find proven techniques for teaching them to take responsibility for their own rooms and to share in the upkeep of your home. You'll also find, in the nutrition section, hints for getting children to eat nutritious, well-balanced meals.

There's no miracle cure for housework, but Chapter 7, Trade Secrets of a Custodian, will help you get the work done faster and with less effort. If your cupboards and closets are hopelessly cluttered, you'll find dozens of ideas on how to throw out the old and create additional space for the new. If your food allowance never seems to last till the end of the month, you'll find scores of tips on how to be a better shopper and how to change your diet to get more food (and better food) for your money.

Each chapter ends with suggestions for applying the ideas and techniques to your own circumstances so that you can make the ideas work for you. And at the end of the book is a special problem-solving section that provides a formula for conquering such home demons as dishes, laundry, mending, and lack of cooperation from family members. Plus there is a final exam which lets you pinpoint your successes as well as the areas that still need work.

You are probably already following many successful home principles. Congratulations! You will be further rewarded as you master even more of the techniques and principles of home organization. This book won't make you rich, and it won't make your work go away. What it will do, if you have a desire to improve your efficiency, is help you get organized so that you can get done what needs to be done and go on to other things. The most satisfying reward of getting control is that it builds self-esteem, which in turn cultivates energy, enthusiasm, and happiness. Nothing breeds success like success.

—Bonnie McCullough

ONE

Making Time by Taking Time to Plan

*1
Go Professional
with a Planning Notebook

Planning takes time but, in the end, saves time and gets better results. The best tool for good time management is the planning notebook. Writing down your commitments, figuring out a work schedule, keeping track of your ideas, and then putting them all together in one place will make this planning process much easier. Professionals pay up to $1,000 to be instructed in these notebook techniques; you can learn and apply the best of these home-management ideas for as little as $4.50.

A planning notebook will give you a visual image of your business. It is so much easier to use a plan on paper than to arrange and categorize it in your mind over and over again. It saves embarrassment over forgotten appointments and helps you protect yourself from overscheduling. If your life is complicated with erratic work hours, meetings, rehearsals, practices, and the like, it will also save your nerves.

The planning notebook that I describe is one that you can make yourself and therefore adapt to your individual needs. It can be divided into sections for monthly and daily planning, and have separate indexes for phone numbers, budget, shopping lists, menus, and so on.

To start your notebook, you will need a pocket calendar or datebook, a small ring notebook, (the same size as the calendar), filler paper, and dividers. Total cost: $4.50. Buy the ring notebook at a discount store and the calendar from a stationery supply center (these calendars are often given out free by banks, greeting card companies, etc.). Carefully take off the outer cover of the pocket calendar and punch holes along the inside crease to fit the rings of the notebook. Put the first few weeks or months of pages behind the first divider in your notebook and you have begun.

CALENDAR SECTION

Use the calendar section to write in *all* your appointments and responsibilities, both social and business. At first you may not think you have enough responsibilities to make this necessary, but you will. There are two secrets to using this appointment calendar:

1. ***Take it with you wherever you go.*** Write down engagements as you hear about them.

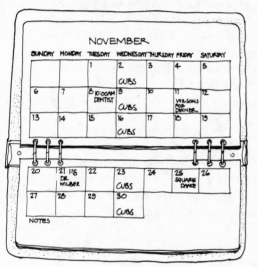

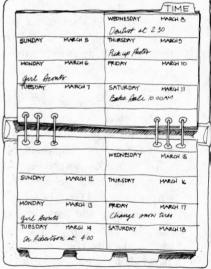

Two examples of a planning notebook, one using a monthly calendar, the other using a two-week calendar.

2. *Check your calendar every day.* Keep it near you in the office, or in the kitchen, or by the phone. As you learn to use your notebook, it will be like having your own private secretary without the cost.

Be sure, though, that the notebook is small enough to carry in your pocket or purse and that you can add pages to it. The calendar section is only the first step in planning your time and your notebook.

Stationery stores carry various types of printed notebooks (see page 6) which will cost more than making the simple one shown on page 4. If you lead a very busy life, one of these books with a full page for every day will be worth the extra investment. (See suggestion list at end of this chapter.) For example, Sharon, a good friend, paid $17 one summer for a commercial notebook. She had three children and a husband enrolled in different baseball teams, each having two practices and one game a week. By the end of the summer, Sharon calculated that the $17 notebook had paid for itself many times over in savings on time, gas, meal preparation, unnecessary phone calls, and, most important, Sharon's nerves. She got hooked on the notebook habit and now uses one all year round.

In addition to the calendar, you will want to include in this section a work chart showing your work plan and regularly scheduled activities. (See Chapter 2 for information on how to set up your work chart.)

PHONE SECTION

Since you will take your notebook with you wherever you go, you'll find it helpful to have a few basic phone numbers written in it. This shouldn't be the same as the family directory you keep by the phone at home: these are the numbers you may need when you are away from home. For example, I was very glad to have the phone number for our Ralph's 66 Station when the car broke down and the telephone book at the public phone booth was missing. You can make your own index tabs within the phone section by cutting away ¼ inch from the outside edge of several pages of filler paper on which you have written three or four alphabet letters (see page 7). Avod using a whole packet of dividers or even a page for every letter of the alphabet because they will make the book too bulky and there are still other important sections to include in your planning notebook.

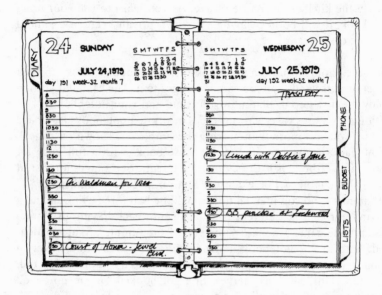

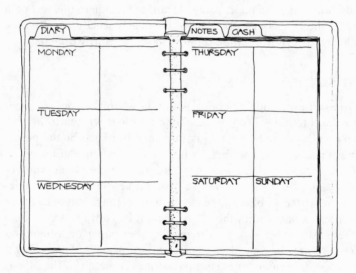

Two examples of commercial notebooks.

MONEY SECTION

Money is the third part of your planning notebook. Use this section to record business expenses or mileage driven on business. This section can also be used to keep track of clothing, household, and food expenses. Try keeping a list of needed groceries, clothing, and toiletries; plus it's a great place to keep a list of favorite seasonal menus, to give you ideas when planning the Food Shopping List.

In the money section of my planning notebook, I plan my monthly budget by listing the projected expenses and a cost estimate on one side of the ledger page. As the purchases are made, I indicate the actual cost and date on the other side. This, however, is not the place for total financial records.

LIST OF LISTS SECTION

The List of Lists section is the second most valuable part of your planning notebook. (The daily calendar takes first place.) This is actually a file of ideas. It doesn't contain notes from an interesting speech, but ideas and plans that come to mind that you may not remember when they can be best used. For instance, when I visit my mother in August, she may mention that Dad would like a popcorn popper. In October, when I am racking my brain trying to think of a gift for his birthday, chances are I won't remember that August conversation unless I have made a note of it. To take it one step further, if I write a date next to "popcorn popper" under Dad's name, I won't be giving him another popper next year.

A smart shopper is always on the lookout for things that might surprise and please the ones he or she loves. For example, if a child is

Make your own index tabs by cutting away ¼″ from the edge of several notebook pages.

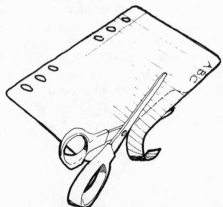

shopping with me, I notice the things she longs for and jot them down. When it comes time for a birthday or holiday, I know exactly what to get as a gift—and save myself hours of shopping time. You can do the same for yourself. When that great desire to have something comes over you, write it down on a Want List. Knowing that it is written in a safe place frees your mind from going over and over it. Then, when you have some extra money, or when someone asks you for a birthday suggestion, you can carefully look at your Want List. You may be surprised that the new lamp you wanted last month doesn't really matter anymore, and the item you truly need most is a new watch. If you are the general purchasing agent for most family clothing or if you like to buy clothes for your boy or girl friends, you'll find it helpful to keep track of everyone's latest shoe, shirt, skirt, or pants size. Your List of Lists section is the perfect place to keep such information. If you find you're starting too many lists, *don't stop making them!* Simply organize this section of your notebook by tabbing the edges of several of the pages (see page 7). You may need to learn to write smaller to help keep the number of pages to a minimum. If you want to succeed, you can't afford to forget things. As ideas pop into mind, jot them down. It's a waste of memory ability to remember what you could just as easily write down. The following is a sample List of Lists that you may find helpful in organizing your ideas:

1. wants—*mine*
2. household needs and decorating wants
3. a page for each boy friend, girl friend, child, or spouse, to keep sizes, gift ideas, and special reminders
4. gift ideas that have been especially well liked
5. books to read
6. projects to be done (sewing, home and auto repair, hobbies)
7. places to go when out-of-town visitors come to your city or when you have a day to yourself or for your family
8. yearly and monthly goals
9. problem areas and tension times to be worked on
10. victory list—to keep track of the good things you have accomplished
11. running project list—see page 13

Practical Application:
1. Prepare a personal planning notebook, including a calendar with weekly or monthly charts or daily pages.
2. Divide the notebook into sections and begin lists for your circumstances to keep track of ideas and plans.
3. Use this notebook for one month, checking calendar daily.
4. At the end of the month, evaluate its usefulness for you.

Recommended Planning Notebooks by Commercial Companies:
The Classic Diary is available in many office supply stores, college book stores, and Bible book shops or can be ordered directly from the publisher: Success Mail Service, P.O. Box 15507, Santa Ana, California 92705. There is a one-time purchase of the ring binder and yearly purchase of calendar refill. It provides a page for each day with hourly time markings, phone, cash, and note sections, including appropriate forms.

The Recordplate line of notebooks and forms is available at most stationers and office supply dealers. They print a "Week-at-A-Glance" notebook in a ring binder with four separate sections and appropriate forms.

The Domestic Goddess Planning Notebook is designed especially to help women organize homemaking responsibilities, appointments, expenses, outside activities, and goals. It is available in some stationery departments or directly from the publisher: Pacific Press, P.O. Box 219, Pierce City, Missouri 65723. Each calendar page has a two-day's "To Do" List (like the one seen on page 11). It is bound by a permanent spiral binding, allows space for daily notes and planning, has a phone section, a place to keep a shopping list (but not a shopping budget), and about six pages for notes.

The Day-Timer planning books are available at some stationery or office supply stores or directly from printer: Day-Timers, Allentown, Pennsylvania 18001. The wallet is purchased once and the calendar refills every year. Each monthly calendar is bound separately with a small spiral and provides two pages for each day with hourly markings. This system is especially good for business men and women who need to keep a permanent expense and time record, and it fits easily in a shirt or jacket pocket.

*2
Getting a Good Start on Today

There was a time when I could be found wandering around my house in a depressed daze for half the morning, trying to decide which of my "necessary" things to do first. I would first begin one project and then start another, and by the end of the morning, I hadn't completed any of them. If you have experienced this same confusion, you can get control of your day by making and following a daily plan.

Begin by establishing an early-morning routine to take care of the everyday essentials: dressing, eating breakfast, cleaning up dishes, packing lunches, getting children off to school, and you and/or your spouse off to work. If you work at home as a student, housewife, or free-lancer, and if you are going to get dressed today, why wait until 2 P.M.? Getting dressed at the beginning of the day can help you get going. Establish a goal time to have the morning routine and pickup finished—perhaps by 9 A.M. if you stay at home or by 7:30 if you work. Then, when you have early appointments or other things you want to do, you won't feel so frustrated and rushed trying to get ready, because getting going will have become a habit. Once the basics are done, you can put more into the rest of the day. It will take time, perhaps even three months, to master your 9 A.M. deadline. If you have a new baby or you are a late riser, your morning-routine goal time might be moved to 10 or 11 A.M.

As you get your day started and complete the morning routine, you will think of things that need doing. *Write them down*, now, for doing later. Many promptings come only once. You will think, "Perhaps I should call Scotty to see if he needs a ride to volleyball practice today." You may notice the refrigerator needs wiping out or the plants need water. Write down these ideas. After you have finished the morning routine, take five minutes to *plan* the rest of the day. As you are planning, refer to your list of to-do-laters from this morning, your weekly work schedule, and your calendar. From these three, you can get an idea of what you want to and need to accomplish today. I call this the To Do List for today. Some people find that starting the next day's planning list before going to bed helps them sleep better. A To Do List can be on a 3 x 5 card, on a scratch paper clipped to the front of your planning notebook, or written on one of the commercial forms from the planning notebooks as illustrated here.

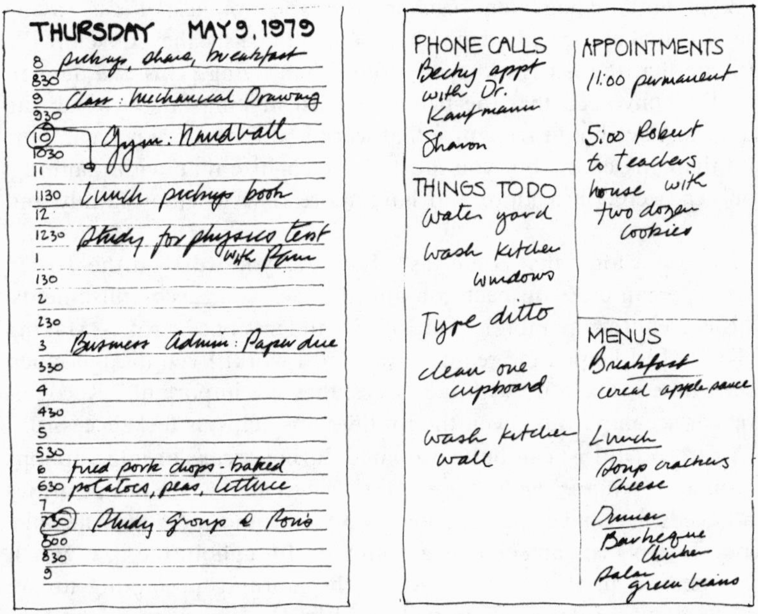

Two variations of the To-Do list. The above form is taken from a notebook available from Fascinating Womanhood, Box 189, Pierce City, Mo. 65723.

If you will be fixing dinner at home, make the menu decision while you are making your plan for today—and this is just as important for the person who is home all day as it is for the person who works. The longer you wait to make the dinner decision, the fewer options you have. And, if you're cooking for yourself, the longer you wait, the less likely you are to cook a full, balanced meal.

As you are writing your To Do List, you will have to organize by priorities. You probably won't get everything done, at least at first, so allow for flexibility. Decide ahead of time which items might be let go until another day. Then choose the right time for each job. (I get more accomplished while "Sesame Street" is on TV than any other time.) Use the biggest block of time for the biggest and most important job and plan to get it done first if possible. When do you have the most energy? That's the time to get the hardest job done. At first you will overplan, but you will soon learn to judge what you can do in one day without neglecting your work or your family.

Some time-management teachers discourage the use of lists, saying that list makers spend so much time writing lists they develop the attitude that the list is more important than living. This is a danger. But I'm convinced that the benefits of list making far outweigh the dangers. You should recognize that work and family are more important than any chore, but you must also recognize that, with planning, you can accomplish more and have more time to enjoy family and friends.

There is a tonic that comes as a bonus as you work on the To Do List. You can cross off each job and thus *see* your accomplishments. This is great for the morale. One of my students once wrote, "Making a To Do List helped me realize how hard I work! Even though much of my time is taken up with the basics, they are important." Recognition for accomplishing even the routine jobs helps us feel successful.

Your To Do List can be reevaluated during breaks or interruptions if you ask *"What is the best use of my time right now?"* Your priorities and needs may have changed since 9 A.M. this morning. Stay flexible. Your To Do List can serve as a reminder throughout the day. When your body is tired, you won't forget the morning prompting to call Scotty about a ride. You can tuck in little jobs like cleaning the fishbowl or watering the plants while heating the soup for lunch. Your list will help you make a better decision about what to do rather than doing just what your eyes happen to see. Another student commented: "I definitely feel a To Do List helps. It keeps my mind freer. I don't forget things to be done, and it is easy to decide what to do next if there is an extra minute or two. Not that it all gets done!"

Try it; you'll like it. The only way to find out if a To Do List works for you is to try using it for five days.

Besides the daily To Do List, you'll want to keep a running list of projects to be worked on in your free or available time. Keep it with your weekly calendar in your planning notebook, or in the list section of your notebook.

These projects on your running list are not the regular weekly tasks, but the extras like repairing your bicycle, sewing the hair on the doll, or planting the garlic. Don't feel defeated if you never get to the end of this list. It is always "running," catching more as the days go by. List things and forget them until you can make time. It is even legal to decide not to do a project and cross it off the list.

Prune Fruit Trees

Renew driver's license
    before birthday

Buy new trash can
Clean garage
Tack down carpet on stairs
Wash and wax car
Call Vetrins to get sofa
Write Mom
Return library books
Balance checkbook

Patch bicycle tires

Running project list

Practical Application:

Try using a To Do List for five days. How do you feel about this five-minute daily planning? Did you get more accomplished than in the past? Did you frustrate yourself by overplanning?

✱3
Scheduling Your Work

Successful businesses everywhere plan their *time* as well as their money. You need to apply this same principle at home, too.

Although it's fun to take a little trip once in a while by flipping a coin at each intersection, we certainly can't go through life traveling by chance. We have important responsibilities, such as children and career. If you take time to plan where you are going and how you will get there, you are more likely to arrive.

Take the worry off your mind by putting it on paper. If the ironing beckons to you while you are scrubbing the floor, be calm; it's already scheduled for Tuesday. No need to worry about the dinner party preparations on Tuesday, because they have been assigned to Thursday.

Now you are ready to learn how to set up a schedule. Let's begin with a schedule for a typical family with children who go to school at regular times and a husband who works days. Then we can adjust for different schedules.

SETTING UP YOUR SCHEDULE

1. *Define your housekeeping goal.* What level of cleanliness would be best for you and your family? Is it your goal to have the kind of home you might see in a fancy magazine, or is it your purpose to organize the home so that you can move easily, find things readily, and live life to its fullest without being tangled in clutter? Do you want your home clean enough just to keep dirt and disease at a minimum? In all probability, you want to be proud enough of your home to invite visitors. You want it decorated enough to be pleasant and restful—a place where you can feel comfortable. Presumably you want it neat most of the time, but not necessarily sterile.

2. ***Decide how much time to spend on cleaning.*** Housecleaning, cooking, child care, laundry, maintenance, and self-fulfillment are all part of home management. Defining what must be done might sound simple—it isn't. Much of your day may be filled with child care and meal preparations or work. Homemakers with families usually spend less than two hours a day actually cleaning, but they have to make those hours count. I asked an elementary school principal how he set up a cleaning program for his school. He said, "We have a specific allotment of work hours. I go through the building with the custodians and decide what has to be done every day (restrooms, drinking fountains, trash, and floors). We put other areas on an alternating schedule." Since our cleaning time is limited at home, we, too, must define the daily necessities and alternate the other chores. A building or home can be "overcleaned" costing you many hours that could be used elsewhere. You may want to set a specific number of hours for cleaning, just as the school does, and then see if you can get the work done in that much time.

3. ***Make a seven-day work chart.*** Fill in your fixed commitments and the basic family happenings for a week: departures, meals, arrivals. From these, a general horizontal time schedule will emerge, showing the structure of your routine, and revealing the best and worst times for different types of work and activities. There will be busy, getting-ready times in the morning. There will be other times during the day when certain jobs seems to fit in better than at other times. For example, dinnertime may be ideal for straightening the kitchen, but not for ironing; the children's nap time might be a perfect time for mending or ironing, but not for vacuuming. Households with school-age children will find time more horizontally structured than those with no children. A school child may leave at 8:30 and get home at 2:30, allowing only six hours in between. These arrival and departure times affect your work. Although it seems confining, you'll notice that people with rigid time structures from children or jobs do seem to get more done as a result of built-in deadlines.

The chart on page 17 shows a horizontal time schedule for a typical family with school-age children, a father who works from nine to five, and a mother who works at home.

4. ***Set aside time for fun***—for yourself, for you and your spouse, and

for you and your family—or it may not happen. If you don't set aside specific time for relaxation, your work and other commitments will take all your time, and life will pass by while you're thinking, "We'll go on a picnic soon." You work hard, and you owe it to yourself to have some fun.

5. *Group the same types of work together* in your schedule as much as possible. I like to arrange three days a week that I can stay home, wear my work clothes, and get everything done. By guarding against interruptions during major work time, I can get more done in a shorter amount of time. Going out for milk at 9 A.M. can take half the morning. Saving the milk stop until later, when I'm out on another errand, not only saves gas but also leaves that whole morning as a three-hour block to get caught up on the washing or to clean the kitchen.

6. *Delegate responsibility.* You don't have to do it all unless you live alone. Every member of the household should carry part of the load. Use the democratic arrangement of sharing. Then, as in business, delegate with no emotional strings attached. Share the fun jobs, too. (See Part 4, Training Apprentices.)

7. *Plan ahead by scheduling.* If your schedule shows music lessons after school, dinner could be ready to pop into the oven before you leave. If you are going to a special luncheon on Tuesday, and Tuesday is laundry day, it may be necessary to start the wash on Monday evening and give up your free afternoon on Wednesday to compensate. If an activity won't fit in on paper, simply say no to it. Overplanning leads to frustration and a short temper.

8. *Value your time.* If time were money, would you waste it? Pretend you are paying yourself a professional wage. Would you want a cleaning person you are paying by the hour to dillydally around? When it's work time, work! On the other hand, even a doctor isn't earning $40 an hour during every waking hour. You don't have to work during all your waking hours either. Part of valuing your time is learning to say no at times.

9. *Stay flexible.* This schedule is made for *you;* you are not its prisoner. You are the executive manager and should be able to make changes to fit special opportunities as they occur. Get in the driver's seat and take control.

HORIZONTAL TIME SCHEDULE

	Monday	Tuesday	Wednesday	Thursday	Friday	Saturday	Sunday

7   Dressed! Hubby off to work, Breakfast and dishes,
    Children's chore time, mother supervises children
8   Children off to school with their lunches made

9   Maintenance time: pick up, put away, straighten, 5 minutes for each room

10 Household work, cleaning or laundry
                        OR
11 Self-fulfillment, service, or personal activities

12 Lunch and clean up

1   Naps for children under 5

2   Work, project, or fun time

3   Children arrive home from school

4   Activities with children: 4-H, music lessons, etc.
    Children's play time. Not a good time for heavy cleaning, mother needs to
       be available
5   Meal preparations, evening chores for children

6   Father arrives home from work
    Evening meal and clean up
7   Family time, listening, helping

8   Family time, meetings, personal projects, homework, etc.

HOW TO APPLY THESE PRINCIPLES TO A SCHEDULE

When I first made a list of work that I had to accomplish, I decided, like the school principal, which jobs had to be done every week and which of those jobs were most important. My schedule needed revising many times because I had a tendency to overplan, especially for Monday. In the beginning, I tried to do all the weekend picking up, baking, and laundry in one day. By the time my husband got home, I was beat. Exhausted! A victim of my own schedule. I hated Mondays!

MY WEEKLY WORK SCHEDULE

Monday	Tuesday	Wednesday	Thursday	Friday	Saturday	Sunday
Major pickup	*Wash*	Women's Auxiliary meeting	Clean one room thoroughly: Two weeks of month will be kitchen.	*Day off*	*Projects*	Day of rest
Make bread	*Iron*				*Yard work*	
Bathroom rugs wash towels	*Mend*		Rotate: wax floor cupboards windows walls furniture stove refrigerator		Help kids w/rooms	Sunday school
					Vacuum basement	
						Church
		Sew or shop			Baths Curl hair Cut hair Plan Sunday dinner	Family time
		Piano lessons	Cub Scouts			
				Date with husband		
Family night at home						Plan next week

18

It worked better for me to allow for a major pickup after the weekend on Monday. Straightening and vacuuming the house on Monday made it easier to accomplish the rest of my work during the week. Now, I also plan to bake bread and thoroughly clean the main bathroom on Monday.

Tuesday makes a good laundry day. I vowed ten years ago never to go to bed on Saturday night until my laundry (including ironing) was caught up, and I haven't. I plan this major task early in the week in case I need a spill-over day. It takes six hours of constant effort to have all the clothing washed, mended, and put away, but I am free of this responsibility the rest of the week because any soiled clothing added to the hamper after Tuesday is part of next week's wash. (See Chapter 18 for secrets on licking the laundry.)

After two hard workdays, things are pretty well in order and I can feel good about taking off Wednesday to attend a church women's auxiliary meeting. Since I'm in my better clothes, I use that afternoon for shopping, appointments, or sewing.

On Thursday, I thoroughly clean one room. Two weeks of the month are spent in the kitchen because it requires so much extra time. By keeping up in the kitchen, I can prepare and clean up meals quickly, leaving my evenings open.

Friday, after I have done the morning routine, is my day for *me*. I took a painting class on Friday mornings for seven years. It was a terrific incentive for me to get my work done early in the week so I could feel free to go. If I have used my work time to play on a previous day in the week, I use part of Friday as a backup.

If Monday is a national holiday, I begin "day one's" work on Tuesday or divide it up into small chunks for the remaining days.

There is never a Monday which I'm not tempted to take off, but I know the penalty: my week crumbles, I get discouraged, and I lose patience. If I put off the necessary upkeep that makes the home run smoothly, *I set myself up for failure.* I also know the rewards of working hard on workdays: the good feeling of being caught up and in control of my time and my life.

A schedule will change with the seasons and stages of your family. You should review it in September and June or when any major change occurs, to make sure you're making the best use of your time. Keep adjusting your plan until it works and you feel comfortable with it. Remember that *you* are the master of your schedule! As with any living thing, there will be constant shifts and changes. Ride the waves. The result will be more free time for yourself and your family, and more time to enjoy the home you've worked so hard to maintain.

The chart on page 18 shows how I've divided the week into a work schedule. Make your own chart and keep it in your planning notebook.

PROBLEM SCHEDULES

The man or woman who works outside the home has so little time left that he or she wants to be free from pressures and restrictions at home, but will have to do the basic maintenance to keep up. Getting it done quickly and as thoroughly as necessary allows time for other things. If you take time to plan, you can get beyond dinner and the dishes. Apply the same principles already mentioned: use a planning notebook, work from a daily To Do List, keep a Running Project List, plan your time, avoid interruptions, and so on.

Eliminate the frills. If most of your hours are committed to someone else (an employer, a baby, or an invalid), there won't be much time left for the more time-consuming parts of home life: baking, gourmet cooking, hobbies, sewing, or gardening. You may have time only for the basic essentials. Work hard on the top-priority items first. Simplify your life. Work smarter by using good work habits (see Part Two, Don't Work Harder, Work Smarter).

Allow preparation time. Often, those who have trouble with over-planning aren't allowing enough buffer time for dressing, travel, or other preparations. When accepting a commitment, take these things into consideration. For example, a student may be able to spend thirty hours in classes, but must remember that thirty hours of class time require sixty hours of study time and that he must also allow time to sleep, prepare food, and take care of clothing.

Share the work. Mary Jane, a working mother, said she asked for two hours on Saturday from each member of the family (including her husband) to do housework. A total of twelve hours was enough to clean their large home. When her own children were too young to clean and after they had gone to college, she hired a willing teenager to dust, vacuum, clean the refrigerator, and so on on Friday afternoons. It took a few hours to train the teen, but for a few dollars a week, Mary Jane had her whole weekend to enjoy and do whatever she chose.

We are sometimes faced with unusual schedules that make planning difficult: illness, a home business, a new baby, children on split sessions at school, a spouse who works nights or has long vacations or is retired. You may not be able to use a weekly schedule, but planning is fundamental. Write down the things that must be done in priority order, and work on the first-priority job before beginning any other. Progress will be slower than if your time were in big chunks, but you can get more done by planning and sticking to one job at a time.

If you have complications with erratic schedules, be very strict on maintenance. Keep things picked up and put away before the house becomes cluttered. Erratic schedules can wreak havoc on your dinner preparations. But if you make the dinner-menu decision early in the morning and post it in the kitchen, your children, if they are old enough, can have dinner well under way by the time you arrive home.

SCHEDULES FOR WORKING PARENTS AND SINGLES

Theoretically, the working parent should have less housework to do. While he or she is away at work, the house stays as is and there won't be as many messes made. This is true only when no one else is home. If the children leave for school after you depart and arrive home before you do, the parent's work multiplies. It is not the nature of children to notice things that need to be done or to carry out chores without adult supervision. The parent is likely to feel like a martyr who is slaving away to put bread on the table while the "ungrateful" kids are loafing at home.

For the working parent to get control at home, the trick is to keep up faithfully with minimum maintenance (pickup, meals, dishes, and laundry) and gain the children's cooperation. (see Chapter 5, MM for More R and R).

Let's look at Larry's family. Larry is a single parent with two children—one daughter, age fifteen, and a son, age eight. Outsiders might assume that Larry could give the traditional "mother" jobs to the girl, who is older. Not true. She cannot keep up in school, mature naturally, and also carry the burden of keeping up a home. He cannot delegate the home responsibility so easily.

Larry also carries an unpleasant memory of his working mother. Weekends were miserable because of her pushing and yelling to finish all the cleaning, scrubbing, washing, ironing, baking, and yard work that she had previously done during the week as a full-time home-maker. Not wanting this atmosphere to dominate his home, Larry made an effort to change in three ways. First, he relaxed the level of housekeeping; second, he set up a program of minimum mainte-nance; and third, he involved the children.

Though he was relaxing the standard, he didn't accept clutter or filth. He gave up daily dusting for a more thorough dusting on Satur-day. Because he kept up with the pickup, each room needed a thor-ough cleaning only every month or two. Painstakingly, Larry had gone through his home eliminating time-taking extras, storing a few treasures and getting rid of the rest. He created a place for everything, making the upkeep much easier.

This father gets his children up with him at 6 A.M. They all dress, eat together, and do a quick pickup through the house. When Larry leaves for work at 7:30, the morning routine is finished. Although the girl is to see the boy off to school, she has been spared breakfast preparation, cleanup, and disciplining her brother through his chores. Even though this first hour of the day is concentrated work, it leaves everyone free until dinnertime.

When he delegated duties to the children, Larry eliminated confu-sion by specifying who, what, when, and how. Then he asked for feedback: "What is your assignment?" Dad also knows that if the job is important enough to be assigned, it deserves a parental inspection. Avoiding the army-sergeant technique, Larry tries to foster a feeling of teamwork and love. By nature, children do not "see" things that need to be done, and if the job isn't theirs they feel no obligation. Many adults haven't even learned this yet—just ask an employer. Be patient with children.

How does Larry handle dinner? We might assume, because he is a man, that he would rely on his daughter, but this family does the meal preparation together between five and six o'clock. Saturday morning they plan the weekly menus, trying to keep them simple but nutri-tious. The menus for the week are then posted so everyone under-stands which ingredients are for meals and which foods can be eaten for snacks.

Rather than plan a strict schedule of duties, Larry leaves his eve-nings open for the activities and needs of his children and himself. Because they have worked together to keep things put away, the rooms are quite free from clutter. On Saturday morning they clean

LARRY'S WEEKLY WORK SCHEDULE

	Monday	Tuesday	Wednesday	Thursday	Friday	Saturday	Sunday
6	Get up, dress, personal grooming.						
6:30	Breakfast together, wash dishes, wipe off counters.						
7	Everyone help with pickup throughout the house, put one batch of clothes in washer.						
7:30							
8							
8:30						Pickup	
9							
9:30						Vacuum, dust	
10						Clean one room	
10:30						thoroughly	
11						Plan menus	
11:30			Work			Shop	
12							
12:30			and				
1							
1:30			School			Individual	
2							
2:30			(time committed to someone else)			and family	
3							
3:30						fun	
4							
4:30							
5							
5:30	Dinner preparations, wash dishes, everyone does pickup.						
6	Dry morning wash and start another batch to wash.						
6:30							
7–9:30	Flexible time for family needs and activities—homework, etc.						

one room thoroughly. The rest of the weekend is saved for individual fulfillment or family fun—they all deserve it!

Even though Larry is a single parent, his technique of planning and minimum maintenance can be applied with equal success to families in which both parents work. The chart on page 23 shows how Larry's weekly work schedule would look.

Practical Application:
Using your scheduling chart, fill in your commitments and work plan. Use it daily. Reevaluate the schedule for flexibility and accomplishments. Keep this weekly work chart in your planning notebook for frequent reference.

*4
For Roommates: How to Divide the Work and Still Like Each Other

When adults live together, how do they arrange the food, the money, and the work and keep everybody happy? In a family, one or both parents automatically decide what work will be done, who is responsible, and how much money will be spent. In group living, you have two or more adults with equal authority. What you need is a *system* that divides the work, the money, and the responsibilities—a system that indicates how much money is needed, who does the work, and when it has to be done.

In an apartment or shared dwelling, you have people with varied backgrounds, standards of cleanliness, nutritional habits, people who have never had to carry their share of responsibility. Invariably, some roommates are more tidy than others. Some overcommit their time with studies, work, or social activities, and others are just plain sloppy. No matter what the cause, the secret is to set up a *system*. The *system* decides.

In a family, everything is shared. In a roommate situation, each adult should be responsible for her or his own clothes, bed, and bath linens. Toiletries, makeup, or shaving supplies should be put back on a specific shelf in the medicine cabinet or in the bedroom. The tub must be cleaned or the shower wiped down after each use. It needs to be understood that "your mother doesn't live here; you'll have to pick up after yourself."

If each person has his or her own bedroom, each can decide his or her own standard of tidiness there. As long as the door will close, it won't affect the others. Sharing a bedroom costs less money but brings added responsibilities. No one should have to put up with a slob (a slob is someone who is messier than you are), making it essential that the minimal level of maintenance be agreed upon. For most, making the bed and keeping things picked up are a must. Putting out-of-season clothing and equipment in a storage area will help keep belongings from migrating into another's territory.

The *system* now divides the rest of the work into responsibilities for two or three teams, allowing for variations in the number of people and the circumstances. You will want to have two, possibly three, work categories: (1) kitchen crew, (2) inside cleaning, and (3) outside chores. Having six people means three teams of two, and four roommates means two teams of two. A group of three roommates might have three teams.

Meet together and agree in detail on what each work category consists of, and post it on a chart. Don't rely on memory! For many, it has been best to have two charts—one for daily and the other for weekly assignments. The following ideas have proven successful in twenty years of apartment sharing, in and out of school. If one individual moves, the new roomie can easily step into the established work divisions.

Team One is in charge of the evening meals and all the related responsibilities for one week. (In a gesture of cooperation, everyone may help with the after-dinner cleanup.) The kitchen crew cooks neatly during the week, cleans the stove and refrigerator on Saturday, and leaves the kitchen ready for the next team. Team Two shouldn't have to wonder how old the leftover spaghetti is or if the tuna salad is safe. Although the hours per week necessary for each team are not equal, the system is fair because everyone takes a turn at the harder tasks.

The remaining housekeeping jobs are divided among the other teams. When your apartment is responsible for outside maintenance, Team Two would have the living-room and bathroom chores and Team Three would take the outside chores such as trash, lawn care, washing windows, snow removal, and so on. If your group does not have outside work, divide the inside jobs between the remaining teams as shown on the following charts.

If the cooking were assigned only one day at a time, no one would feel the direct responsibility to scour the broiler pan or keep the kitchen clean. It is also easier for those who are going to cook to plan the meals and buy the food, staying within the budget and keeping

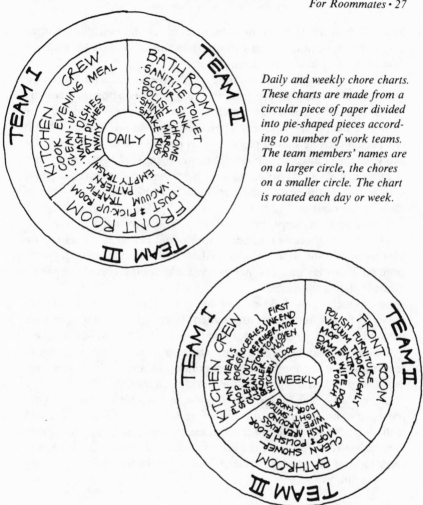

Daily and weekly chore charts. These charts are made from a circular piece of paper divided into pie-shaped pieces according to number of work teams. The team members' names are on a larger circle, the chores on a smaller circle. The chart is rotated each day or week.

the meals nutritionally balanced. On your heavily scheduled days, you can trade off with your partner if you are a working team. Or, if you cook alone, put a roast and potatoes in the crock pot for dinner before you leave, plan a quick meal of meatballs in the pressure cooker, or buy fried chicken on the way home.

There is flexibility in this plan. If one party has more money than time, she could pay someone to do her share of the chores. This functions best when the money comes from separate incomes. Knowing your exact duties months in advance can allow you to trade off days or weeks when opportunities come.

Take the madness out of money by agreeing on who pays how much for what. Will the rent, utilities, and deposits be divided equally or will they be separated and each roommate pay one? Under whose name will the phone be listed? These decisions sound so simple, but if one person feels he should pay only part because he has been gone for two weeks, you have a problem. The apartment scene gets more complicated when you try to coordinate purchases of furniture or major appliances. In this case, one person may need to take the role of "lead" roommate.

The same ideas apply to food costs. You may need a rule—pay whether you're there or not. Set a fair amount per week. (We lived on $4 a week, but inflation has changed all that.) Should one person be gone on Thursday and another every weekend, the cost of preparing meals is almost the same.

Be specific in your food-money decisions. Talk about who will buy the extra food when guests are invited. If the kitchen crew goes over the budget, who pays the additional amount? What about lunches? Will everyone buy his or her own except on weekends? Are the cooks responsible for buying breakfast supplies and milk, or will you each buy your own? And who pays for cleaning supplies?

Living together should be fun. Decide on a system and let it be your regulator. Anticipating problems before they happen minimizes bad feelings on the other side of a solution. This system, or any organized system, insures that the work gets done and that no one person has to carry most of the burden, while still allowing the flexibility of trading responsibilitites.

Practical Application:

Call a meeting with your roommates to set up a system for the work responsibilities. Make a list of the chores that need to be done daily and weekly, and then divide the tasks among the two or three teams. Make and post chore charts reflecting your decisions.

Discuss and agree upon the financial arrangements. It's also a good idea to write down these money agreements and not leave them to memory.

TWO

Don't Work Harder, Work Smarter

✻5
MM for More R and R

Have you ever had to stay at home, lock the doors, and take the phone off the hook to shovel out after a PTA Pancake Breakfast? This is the Typical Crash Crisis System of too many busy people, and it's doomed to failure. They let the house go while taking care of a Scout activity or church social. Then they dig out. When more than one outside activity occurs in a week, the house is unlivable. The husband or wife resents the "service" that is given in the name of compassion or career, and tension develops.

There is a better way! You can put an end to frazzled nerves and short tempers by developing your own MM system.

There is no such thing as a miracle cure, but MM (minimum maintenance) can set you free by 9:30 in the morning or have you ready to leave for work on time—and that means with breakfast wiped away, children dressed, dinner planned, and the clutter cleared. The MM system is simple to use. It calls for daily, organized house "keeping" rather than weekly or seasonal house-cleaning ordeals. MM will give you more R & R (rest and relaxation) time for you. Here's how to do it:

1. ***Begin with the basic pickup plan.*** Put on an apron with pockets, check the time on your watch, and give each room five minutes before starting any major project of the day. You put away, straighten up, and wipe off. Where do you start? There is an art to knowing where to begin. What does a caller at your door see first? Pick up this area and it will not only give your spouse, children, and guests a feeling of neatness, it will also give you a feeling of pride and accomplishment, no matter what the rest of the house looks like. Begin with the biggest items, such as bed, newspapers, or kitchen table. Work your way down to the smallest objects, which

can be collected in your apron pockets. Work with gusto. It's amazing what you can do in only five minutes, but don't stay longer. (You can allow yourself fifteen to twenty minutes in the kitchen if it needs it.)

This is only the basic maintenance. When it is finished, you can begin the day's project, whether it be work, school, or shopping. You can leave the house knowing that when you return, everything will be in order. If your house is in order, it says, "You are successful. You are making progress." If you come back to dirty dishes, unemptied ashtrays, and last night's newspapers, your house says to you, "You're a failure. You'll never catch up!" The pickup process is rewarding and generates success. This positive reinforcement gives you more energy to go on. It's a good feeling to walk into a room and see it in order.

2. ***Don't start cleaning too deeply during your morning run-through.*** This isn't the time to scrub the whole kitchen floor or clean out the refrigerator. When you see jobs that need doing, jot them down on a project list for later, during cleaning time. If you're thinking you can say good-bye to thorough cleaning forever, remember that MM is no miracle. It is a method for keeping clean what you've spent valuable time and energy to get thoroughly clean.

3. ***Don't let the needs of others control your life.*** Suppose a friend calls and says, "I'm desperate, can you help me make posters today?" It's for a good cause. This friend has helped you before. *But don't just drop your world.* Do the maintenance first. (Work before pleasure.) A home can run smoothly for a long while on minimum maintenance. Throw the meat and potatoes in a crock pot, dress the children, wipe away breakfast, quickly pick up through the house while a batch of clothes is in the washer, and you can be ready to go by 9:30. Going straight from the breakfast table to posters is asking for a backfire at about five, when you'll be thinking, "I hate this housework; I can't ever do what I want." Anyone who chooses to come back to undone chores *should* hate it. Learn to reward yourself after, rather than before, your MM is finished.

4. ***Make the dinner decision early.*** The longer you wait, the fewer choices are available. No preparation yet—just get it settled. Five o'clock is too late to discover you need to take something from the freezer or stop at the store.

5. *When the enthusiasm strikes to clean, don't make the mistake of starting in the cupboard, closet, or drawer.* Start from the outside in. Take care of the clutter scattered around the room before digging into the chest of drawers. Starting with the closet first makes a double mess. You'll get discouraged and quit before either job is finished. Begin from the outside in—clutter before closet.

6. *Categorize your household items.* You might ask, "If the drawers are messy, where will I put everything?" Put the items in category areas where they will be used or stored: gardening supplies to the garage, arts and crafts to the game room, Cub Scout materials to a closet. The categories that you originally create may not be the most efficient, but start by grouping. Then get more specific. I know one mother of five who is so involved with organizing her cupboards that the "living" parts of her home are stacked with "I'll-get-to-it-someday" items. Putting every bottle, button, and bobbin in its place takes all her time. By practicing MM and taking thirty minutes to do this grouping before she begins the cupboards, she would have her entire home looking neat and tidy—not just the cupboards and closets.

7. *Learn to pick up before the mess becomes monstrous.* This applies to every member of the family—especially children. After each play period and just before eating or going to bed, allow time to pick up.

8. *Make the picking-up process a habit.* At first it will take great effort, but it will soon become second nature.

Spend the first hour of the day picking up, and get in the habit of picking up during other spare moments of the day. Make cleaning up and putting away a part of every task, whether it's finished or not. In school shop or sewing class, you put your materials and tools away in a tote tray. It took only two minutes. What would have happened if five classes of twenty students each left their things out because they were going to work on it tomorrow? About the same kind of thing that happens at home: chaos! Magic markers left out invite a two-year-old to decorate the walls. Yesterday's dishes take twice as long to wash. No one else can use the desk if it's still covered with papers. Why leave the sled in the backseat of the car for two weeks?

Keeping up with MM (minimum maintenance) means there's hope. Develop the habit of putting things away while they're still in your hand and before going on to something else. My mother-in-law dropped by one Monday morning at 8:30 and exclaimed, "It looks like you've been up cleaning all night!" My five minute pickup had worked! I had barely finished washing the dishes and carrying an armload of debris out of the living room. Taking time to plan and pick up in the morning pays off at 4:30 in the afternoon, giving you extra time, just like passing through a time zone.

Practical Application:

There is an art to discovering where to begin work and how much to start without making a bigger mess than you had in the beginning. Let's see what you have learned.

It is just after the heavy Christmas season, and you have let some things in your home slide while you worked on crafts, gifts, and programs. A special friend came to town for a week. Since there's little money, you decide to invite her and a few friends to lunch at your home, rather than go out. Your week is already full of important responsibilities. Allowing time for cooking, you have only four hours left to clean. What will you clean? Where will you begin?

Your guests are really coming to see each other, not your house, but you are sensitive and this might spoil the whole occasion for you. First, ask yourself—where will they be? What will they see? Clean most completely in these top priority areas and give the other rooms a quick pick up. Work on the most obvious—biggest to smallest. Start in the bedroom only if that's where you plan to serve lunch.

*6
Plan Ahead

HAVE THE NECESSARY EQUIPMENT

Every business needs the right tools and equipment to deliver good service. How long would it take a carpenter to build a house without a power saw? Who could afford to hire that carpenter? The right supplies and appliances will also improve your efficiency at home. The president of a large women's service group told me she waited eight years before getting a long telephone cord (which cost $12). She lost hundreds of hours because she couldn't get more than five feet from the phone. She couldn't turn down the burner, reach a book, or empty the dishwasher.

As you get new equipment, adapt your work habits and be certain you are using it correctly. It took me longer to load and empty the dishwasher at first than it did to wash the dishes by hand. Give yourself a "learning time." Anything new or different that you do—whether it's trying a new recipe or using a microwave oven—will take longer in the beginning. It is as though you have to carefully lay down railroad tracks so that later you can operate without steering, checking, or concentrating. I was afraid I had been unwise in my dishwasher investment, but after mastering the motions, I considered it my most valuable appliance—next to the washing machine.

Many businesses go bankrupt every year because of mismanagement. Home managers can go bankrupt, too, if they buy more equipment and appliances than they really need. For example, one of my neighbors, Roy, was a tool-aholic. He didn't stop to consider the difference between the necessary tools and the nice-to-have tools. He once bought a whole railroad carload of pipe because it was cheaper in larger quantities. In his business, it would have taken him ten years to use up that much pipe. His capital and assets couldn't carry that kind of expenditure, and he went bankrupt.

The chief cause of unhappiness is giving up what you want most for what you want at the moment. Home managers can overbuy in their home business. Very few homes have a budget that will allow unlimited spending for supplies and equipment. It is your job to manage this fund and to carefully weigh the cost, time savings, and actual need for each proposed investment. Before buying, ask: Do I have to have it? How did my ancestors do without it? How much time will it save? Will something I already have do instead? With such careful managing, Roy would have avoided failure.

MAKE REPAIRS EASY: HAVE THE NECESSARY SUPPLIES

Benjamin Franklin wrote in *Poor Richard's Almanac,* "A little neglect may breed great mischief . . . for want of a nail the shoe was lost; for want of a shoe the horse was lost; and for want of a horse the rider was lost." Plan ahead. Have basic supplies on hand so you can make repairs before an item is damaged even more. If you have a supply of various colors of thread, a small hole in a knit shirt can be sewn closed before it becomes a long run. With a screwdriver close by, the knob on a chest of drawers can be screwed back in before it is lost. If the equipment is handy, repairs will be so much easier. Here's a list of basics you should have on hand:

1. a variety of glues for glass, paper, metal, and wood (one glue won't do)
2. pencils, note paper, stapler, paper clips, thumb tacks, matches, rubber bands, scissors, masking tape, transparent tape, string, safety pins, and straight pins
3. heavy-duty strapping tape for mending the backs of books, a roll of good transparent tape for mending book pages (the life of children's books can be doubled by mending when damage is just beginning—and kids expect parents to be able to mend anything)
4. a permanent magic marker, liquid embroidery-paint tube, and printed cloth name tags to put your name on all items likely to leave the house (even the broom)
5. a hammer, an assortment of screwdrivers, and a pair of pliers

(an extra set kept in the kitchen will save many steps to the garage or toolbox)

6. a *wide* variety of colored thread—one to two dozen spools—for mending (nothing kills the impulse to mend quicker than not having the right color of thread—see chapter 18 for more instructions on mending)
7. stationery, postcards, stamps, address book, and pens
8. a plunger and length of wire or coat hanger to free clogged drains, (you can just smell the problems these can avoid)
9. an assortment of nails, screws, washers and bolts
10. clear nail polish—that old standby—to stop runs in nylons

GIFT SHELF

In a remote, out-of-the-way corner, keep a few gifts for birthdays, weddings, and other special occasions. This can save hours of frenzied shopping if your child receives a party invitation or if you're unexpectedly invited to a wedding and don't have the cash or the time to run out and buy something. By getting an item on sale, you can give something nicer than your budget would normally allow. *Caution:* Don't get too many gifts ahead. Styles and stages change.

BORROWING

We can't all have everything, so it is nice to be able to use someone else's tools and equipment. I don't mind sharing my possessions, but it gripes me when someone borrows something and it doesn't come back. If the borrower forgets where it came from, it is gone forever.

To keep borrowed items from being absorbed into your household belongings, try these suggestions: make sure the loaner's name is on it. Return the item in better condition than it was received if possible (press the pattern or costume, wipe off the lawn mower, replace the bit on a drill). Be willing to repair it or buy a replacement if you damage it. Never integrate borrowed items into your own. When you borrow an item, tell the loaner how long you think it will take and then make every effort to return it promptly. If you are not yet finished with it, call the owner and ask for an extension; give the reason and set a new deadline.

If you are the loaner, a few precautionary measures will increase your chances of getting the object back: *Put your name on it!* Set a courteous deadline. Keep a record of loaned items (in an inconspicuous place). If the suggested deadline passes, make a gentle reminder—even the most organized people slip once in a while.

SYSTEMATIC MAIL HANDLING

Think of the times you have opened a letter and thought, "I should do something about this." When you picked it up again, it was too late or too embarrassing to do anything about it (like the pile of Christmas cards you intended to answer but finally threw away in June). This can be avoided if you make a decision as the mail comes in, and handle it only once.

Your mail will fit one of the following categories:

1. *Reply immediately.* A postcard sent today is better than a letter well intended. Take just a moment to do it today. As school notes and letters arrive, mark down meetings, parties, receptions, and responsibilities on your planning calendar, noting the time and address, and throw the reminder away.

2. *Answer within the week.* Jot it down on your Running Project List.

3. *File bills.* Designate a spot for bills to stay until payday.

4. *Keep for future reference.* Your important papers need a metal box. Less important papers and check receipts can be kept in a shoe-box or accordion file folder. (See page 64, How to Set Up a Home Filing System That Works.)

5. *Put in wastebasket.* Your best friend. Use it more often than all the others. Decide now if you are going to enter the sweepstakes drawing or throw it in the bucket. Don't set it in a pile, only to have to go through it later.

In my youth, I was taught to say thank you twice, in two different ways. The first thank you is usually a verbal expression—"Thanks for the lovely dinner." Writing a note is often appropriate for a second conveyance of your appreciation. After you get home from the party, write a quick note of thanks while the memory is still warm. It can be done faster than your spouse can brush his or her teeth, and you will gain a reputation for being prompt and thoughtful. By planning ahead, you can always have cards and stamps on hand. (If you take the time to help your children do the same, it will nurture the virtue of gratitude.)

HOUSEHOLD RULES

Keep a list of your household rules and family routines in case someone should have to come in and take over your home for a few hours or days. When is the milk delivered? What day is the trash picked up? On a bulletin board, post an emergency list of phone numbers for police, fire, ambulance, doctor, dentist, poison-control center, pastor, neighbors, schools, and work. At the bottom, include basic house rules, for example: "I don't want my children to jump on the trampoline or ride their bikes while I am away." It is all written for whomever is in charge. You can be away with your mind at ease.

JUST FOR TODAY

Here is a quick check to help you see how well you are applying the principles of planning, and good work habits. Rate each question from 0 to 5, five being the highest and best.

1. _____ I got up on time.
2. _____ Each family member was dressed and groomed before 9:00 A.M.
3. _____ Every room was picked up (5 minutes' worth) before beginning the day's project.
4. _____ I made a To Do List and worked from it during the day.
5. _____ I decided what would be served for dinner before 10:00 A.M.
6. _____ Our meals today contained servings from the basic groups: 2 milk, 2 meat, 4 fruit and veg., and 4 grain products.
7. _____ My schedule didn't become more important than my job or my family.
8. _____ I didn't overplan and get frustrated.
9. _____ Dinner was served at the appointed time.
10. _____ I lovingly listened to each child tell about her or his day.
11. _____ The children helped in some way with the care of our home.
12. _____ I gave more praise than criticism.
13. _____ Before the meal preparations, I cleaned off the counter and work area.

14. _____ As I was fixing meals, I had the sink full of hot water and washed preparation dishes and utensils.
15. _____ I forced myself to do one thing I had been putting off.
16. _____ I showed appreciation to someone other than family members.
17. _____ I told each member of my family that I loved him or her.
18. _____ I had a few minutes all my own.

*7
Trade Secrets of a Custodian

"When I hire a woman who has been a homemaker to professionally clean a building, she works like she does at home and we never make any money," says Arlo Luke, president of Varsity Contractor, Inc., a national custodial company. "Women in the home haven't changed their methods of cleaning—they are very inefficient. For instance, I hired a woman to clean a building which we bid at three and a half hours per day. It was taking her six hours and she swore it couldn't be done *well* in less. It was taking forty-five minutes just to clean one restroom. When I showed her how it could be done in fifteen minutes, she was absolutely speechless. My job was every bit as clean, sanitized and shining. She was using old methods—slow methods, like milking a cow by hand instead of using a milking machine."

Approach your home work with the same efficiency you would if you were a professional and this were a high-paying job. The ideas in the following pages will have to be applied one or two at a time. Habits are like a bundle of sticks—you can't break them all at once. Learning new habits will be very painful, but using these principles may just change your life.

SECRET #1: PREVENTION

The custodian's first consideration in saving money is prevention. A major technique is to prevent dirt from entering the building by providing mats to collect the dirt. This is accomplished by placing a rough mat outside to collect the heavy dirt, and a softer, nylon-rubber mat just inside the door to catch dirt from each person's first few steps. Good doormats will save time and work at home, too.

The following is a list of prevention hints that will help eliminate some of your daily work:

1. If everyone in a family were to wear some of his or her outfits twice, it could save an hour on wash day. (But the neighbors might talk.)
2. Bibs for babies keep them clean and make them easier to love.
3. Children's bed sheets could be changed every other week.
4. Buy a doormat if you can't get your family to remove their shoes in the entry.
5. Wipe down the bathroom tile after each use and there will never be a scum buildup.
6. To prevent loss, put your family's name on anything that is likely to leave the house: purses, tools, sports equipment, books, coats, toys. (You can always deny that the kid is yours.)
7. Don't have pets.
8. Don't eat in the wrong rooms.
9. Before buying something, decide if you are willing to give the time necessary for its upkeep.
10. Wash dishes after each meal, before food dries on plates.

SECRET #2: THE CLEANING BASKET

If a professional custodian had to return to the supply closet every time he or she needed a dust cloth, a sponge, or a can of disinfectant, no one would want (or be able to afford) his or her services. To save time, steps, and money, professional cleaners always carry their supplies with them in a basket or bucket.

This same rule can be applied to your own techniques of cleaning at home. Over a period of a month or a year, a cleaning basket can save countless hours and will put an end to those unnecessary trips up and down the stairs, and to and from the utility closet.

Your cleaning basket can be anything from a wicker basket to a rubber or plastic pail, but it makes your work easier if the basket is wide, with low sides and a flat bottom so each bottle, can, or brush can be seen and easily reached. The following is a list of the basics to have in your basket:

1. general cleaner
2. glass cleaner
3. disinfectant
4. all-purpose rug spot cleaner

} each labeled and in squirt bottle (aerosols cost too much!)

5. furniture polish
6. sponge with *mild* abrasive on one side
7. cleanser
8. several soft cloths
9. paper towels
10. plastic bag to collect trash in

Taking the maid basket as you go in to clean a room will encourage a more thorough job. Keep the inventory of cleaning supplies and equipment simple and evaluate their effectiveness periodically. For instance, the cleaning cloth itself has as much to do with the results as the solution. Soft, absorbent cottons such as diapers or terrycloth clean better than tightly woven synthetics.

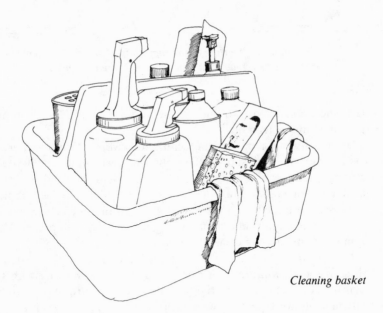

Cleaning basket

SECRET #3: DIRECTION AND TECHNIQUE

With your cleaning supplies in hand, you're ready to start—but professionally, with direction—*clockwise*. Starting at the supply closet and ending there, go through the building (your house or apartment) a room at a time. The basic idea of the clockwise system is to start at the

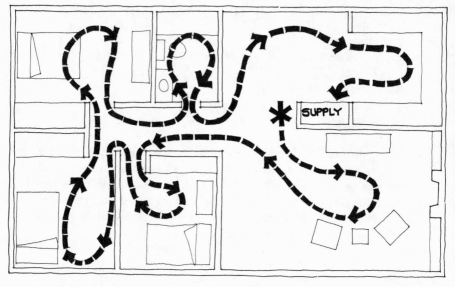

Work with direction. *Starting at the supply closet and ending there, go through your home a room at a time in a clockwise direction.*

back and bring the dirt to the *front* so you are never moving from a dirty area into a clean one.

Dusting also has a movement technique: *always follow your hand.* If you are right-handed, start at the right and dust to the left; if you're left-handed, start at the left and dust to the right. By following your hand, you won't spread dust over places you've already wiped. Professionals also use the technique of dusting high places (picture frames, door jambs, etc.) first, and then moving to lower areas to prevent dust from dropping all over cleaned areas.

After dusting, use a general cleaner for metal or tough plastic finishes, and use furniture polish on wood furniture (moving with the grain). Be careful to use the right cleaner for each surface (try using a different color or type cloth with each cleaner to prevent such mixups as wiping your mirror with the furniture-polish cloth).

As you work around the room, pay special attention to finger marks on doors, light switches, and door handles. Then stop and look. Are things like the chairs and pictures straightened?

Now vacuum the room, starting at the back of the room and working toward the door. Carpet spots should be sprayed with carpet cleaner and blotted carefully (rubbing may spread the stain). Heavy traffic areas, such as halls and entrances, need to be vacuumed daily, but rooms with very little use may need a thorough vacuuming only every week or two.

What about the most sensitive public-used area, the restroom? It calls for special, daily care, but can be done in a very few minutes. Here, again, you'll move clockwise, bringing the dust and debris *forward* from the back to the front in order to go from a cleaned area into a dirty one. Always clean from high places to low places.

Professionals get a fresh, pleasant smell from cleanliness, not scents. Spray the entire outside surface of the toilet with disinfectant and let it stand a moment while you lift the seat, flush the toilet and clean the bowl, being sure to swab the inside and under the lip of the bowl. (A sponge brush works better in the toilet bowl than a bristle brush.) Starting at the top and working down, wipe down all the outside surfaces of the toilet with paper towels, being sure to polish the metal fixtures and wipe behind the toilet and around the bottom of the bowl.

Clean the bathroom in a clockwise direction, moving dust and dirt from back to front in order to go from clean area to dirty area.

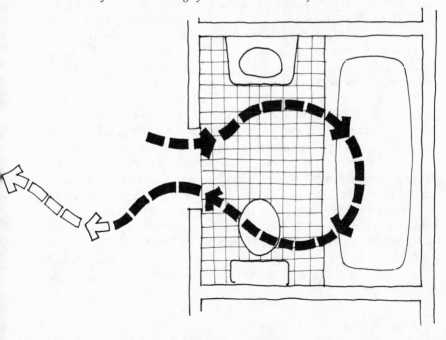

Sinks and tubs should be lightly scoured with a dab of cleanser, rinsed, and then the fixtures polished. Replace the toilet tissue. Custodians suggest the paper unroll toward the person, not toward the wall, and that the cardboard tube be flattened so it doesn't unroll too easily and thus waste paper.

Dust door and mirror edges, and clean any spots on the walls, door, and light switch. Don't forget to sanitize the door handle! Wipe the floor, catching the corners.

What about walls? Try the two-bucket method. Fill one bucket with warm water and a little general cleaner. Keep the empty bucket close by. Dip the sponge only partway into the cleaning solution to avoid drips. Starting at the top of the wall, cover a three-foot-square section of wall with the solution. Wipe clean with a soft dry cloth. Squeeze dirty sponge into *empty* bucket, dip into clean solution, and repeat. This keeps the solution clean, thereby saving supply costs, and gets the walls cleaner. When you're finished, the empty bucket will be full of dirty water and the cleaning solution will still be clean.

And those stubborn wall spots? The secret is patience. If the mark won't come off with the general cleaner, try these professional tips: with a damp soft cloth and a dab of cleanser-paste (cleanser plus a little water), slowly, carefully, and lightly rub the mark. Most cleansers are very abrasive and can take off the finish, leaving a light spot where the mark was if you rub too hard. When the mark is gone, the professional lightly blends the cleanser into the surrounding area.

How do custodians clean windows? Watch them. They don't use squirt bottles or newspapers. They use a squeegee with a good rubber edge that extends beyond the metal edges of the squeegee frame. (You can buy one in your hardware store.) They put half a capful of dishwashing liquid in a bucket of warm water as a wetting agent and wet the window with a sponge. They wipe the squeegee across the top and side edges to prevent drips and cut the water bead that adheres to the edge. They pull the squeegee either down or across the wet portions of the window. (If you draw the squeegee across on the inside of the window and down on the outside of the window, you can easily tell which side of the window still has streaks.) After each motion, custodians wipe the blade with a *damp* (never dry) sponge to keep the edge lubricated. They wipe the ledge with a paper towel, and the job is finished.

You can use a squeegee in the same way as the professionals. If

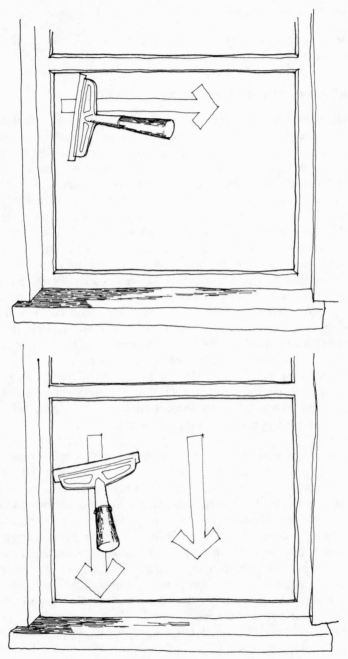

Wipe across top and side to cut out bead of water. Then pull either down or across to wipe off rest of water.

your windows have screens, brush or wash the screens so the first little breeze doesn't get your windows dirty again.

SECRET #4: PRIORITIES AND APPEARANCES

"When the entrance and restrooms of a building are clean, one naturally assumes the rest of the building is also clean," reports Mr. Luke. This is also true at home. Families and guests are affected by what they see when they enter. How much time and attention do you give the areas that are first seen in your home? What do guests see as they walk in the door? The kitchen table? The hat and coat rack? The playroom? The piano? Where does your family enter? After a hard workday, do you and your spouse enter through the laundry room? How does this make you feel about yourself and your home?

When custodians can't get a whole building clean, they give special care to the restrooms and entry. Even though you can't have everything clean, certain rooms have first priority. The entry has top rating because of its effect on all who see it. The kitchen ranks next in line, because it is a heavy work area and needs to be reasonably clean for the sake of your family's health. The bathrooms must be clean for the same reasons you want the restrooms in a restaurant clean.

The bedrooms, family room, den, and game room are usually secondary. The workrooms, utility area, and garage could take third place in your home. According to your circumstances, decide which rooms are most important and should be tackled first.

By taking the time to assign uses to each room in your house or apartment, you can better meet the needs of your family—and help prevent such unnecessary calamities as raspberry-pop stains on your satin bedspread, dog hairs on the velvet chair, and race-car ruts on the glass coffee table. Room definitions can give baby a place to eat and spill, siblings a corner to play, and parents the comfort of knowing one room in the house is at its best. Your family may need a place for quiet music practice or study away from the TV. One wise mother lets her children cut, paste, color, and paint at the breakfast nook, which can be easily cleaned up, rather than deny them creative experiences because she can't control the mess.

Together, in a family council, talk about your needs and activities. Decide the purposes for each room of the house. Write them down so there are no misunderstandings (see the sample forms on pages 50–51).

After choosing the purposes for a room, stick to them—and demand the cooperation of all family members (and pets). Deciding the uses for each room, getting cooperation, and carrying through with these resolutions are the major parts of preventive housekeeping. Grease is harder to clean off the shag carpet than a vinyl floor.

Laura was lamenting that her bedroom was the house catchall. As she began her house reform, she wanted to have at least one room neat, and she chose her bedroom to be that place. After all, she shares the room with her husband; they discuss things and rest there. Her room definition stated that this bedroom was for dressing and sleeping. Other places were found for the Girl Scout materials, library books, mending, and family TV. No more waking up in the morning to waist-high clutter; it was easier to start the day. Laura's bedroom became a place of refuge, not refuse, and as she worked on conquering other parts of her home, the neat bedroom gave her an incentive to get it all that way.

SECRET #5: SET A DEFINITE CLEANING SCHEDULE

Most professional custodians work according to a list of specific daily, weekly, and monthly duties agreed to in their contract. For example: "The light fixtures will be cleaned annually, the first week of the fourth month; the windows will be washed in May and October." A list of these duties is often posted inside the janitorial closet. Whoever is working, whether it be the regular or a substitute, knows *exactly* what must be done. This technique will work at home, too. Try writing a job description for each room in your home. As the home manager, you decide what must be done and how often. Regular, gentle cleanings are easier on your furnishings than sporadic, tough scourings.

The job description saves misunderstandings with your children and can help them self-evaluate. It is a measure for parents to use, taking them out of the "bad-guy" spot, giving the child the responsibility for checking each detail on the chart. On page 52 are the cleaning specifications for our home. We planned them on our room-purpose charts (see page 51) typed them on index cards and tacked them in the closets.

ROOM PRIORITIES AND CLEANING SPECIFICATIONS

Room:_____

Room Priority: Top_____ Secondary_____ Third_____

Purposes for this room: (Uses allowed and not allowed, items and
activities that belong here)

1.

2.

3.

4.

5.

6.

7.

CLEANING SPECIFICATIONS:

Daily:

1.
2.
3.
4.
5.
6.

Weekly:

1.
2.
3.
4.
5.

Quarterly:

1.
2.
3.
4.
5.

ROOM PRIORITIES AND CLEANING SPECIFICATIONS

Room:___Living room_____

Room Priority: Top_____X_____ Secondary_____ Third_____

Purposes for this room: (Uses allowed and not allowed, items and activities that belong here)

1. receive guests

2. dressy room of house

3. used for reading, visiting, piano practicing

4. used for family-council meetings

5. not allowed: roughhousing, eating, crafts

6. not a drop-off for school books or coats

CLEANING SPECIFICATIONS:

Daily:

1. books and toys put away
2. piano closed, bench under
3. cushions straight
4. newspapers put away
5. traffic areas vacuumed

Weekly:

1. thoroughly vacuum, dust, and polish furniture
2. take newspapers to garage
3. wipe around door, knobs, and light switches
4. thoroughly vacuum carpet

Quarterly:

1. vacuum drapes
2. wash windows
3. clean light fixtures
4. dust ceiling corners

CLEANING SPECIFICATIONS (TO BE TACKED IN CLOSETS):

Front Room
Daily:
Put away books and toys.
Close piano; put bench under.
Straighten cushions.
Put newspapers neatly under table
   in far corner.
Vacuum traffic areas.

Weekly: (Saturday)
Vacuum carpet.
Dust all furniture.
Take newspapers to garage.
Damp-wipe around door.
Shake rugs.
Sweep porch.

Bathroom
Daily:
Pick up all hair equipment and
   straighten counter.
Pick up toys and clothes.
Straighten towels.
Scour sink and polish chrome.
Wipe off back of toilet.
Shake rug.

Weekly:
Scour toilet bowl.
Wash towels.
Wash brushes and combs.
Polish mirrors.
Sweep and mop floor.

Bedrooms
Daily:
Make bed.
Pick up clothes.
Fold and put away pajamas.
Keep top of bed and chest neat.

Weekly:
Dust.
Vacuum.
Straighten drawers.
Change bed sheets.
Damp-wipe around door.

Family Room
Daily:
Pick up toys and books.
Straighten blankets and pillows.

Weekly:
Vacuum carpet.
Wipe TV and around doors.
Dust.

Kitchen
Daily:
Rinse and put dishes in
   dishwasher.
Refill cold drinking water.
Cover leftovers and put in
   refrigerator.
Wash pans and serving bowls.
Dry pans and serving bowls.
Shake rugs.
Sweep floor.
Scour and polish sink.
Wipe off counters and table.
Put away chairs.
Fold down table.

ADDITIONAL HINTS FOR MAKING
HOUSEWORK EASIER

Go to work on workdays. The hired laborer who takes off work to go fishing very often will get fired. The business person who constantly neglects her or his business will end up a failure. The home manager who decides not to work on workdays because he or she is not in the mood is cheating, and it will eventually show. One nice thing about being the home manager is that you can schedule your housework around your job, vacations, appointments, or opportunities. (But every day shouldn't be a work day; see Chapter 3, Scheduling Your Work.) You might just as well accept the fact that it takes a minimum number of work hours to keep your head above water.

If you consider yourself a hard worker at home but can't seem to get everything done, keep a log of your time for a few days. Every thirty minutes, write down how you spent your time. You'll be surprised! Maybe you are not working as much as you thought. It's not the work that makes you tired, it's the undone work. If you find you have more work than one person can possibly do, then you'll not only have to use good work habits but also seek ways to eliminate part of the work or get help.

"But I don't like to clean house!" Sometimes you have to force yourself to do something because it needs to be done. Why wait two years to wash the kitchen ceiling when it is actually a one-hour job? We tend to put off the less pleasant things, and procrastination becomes a habit. Force yourself to prove it can be done. Offer yourself a fun incentive or time off. If you become paralyzed because the job is so big, divide it into small parts. Finishing a job is wonderful medicine; behaviorists call it a self-reinforcing action. It is fuel for another task. Just going to work on workdays will improve your attitude toward work that must be done. "The secret of happiness is not in doing what one likes, but in liking what one has to do," said James M. Barry. After several experiences of that rewarding feeling from getting the unpleasant job out of the way, of relief from its pressure, you will have acquired the do-it-today habit, a major key to success.

Dress appropriately. If you walked into a sales-training seminar today, the first thing you would learn would be to dress like you are already successful in your profession. How does a successful home manager dress? Whom do you picture in your mind? Not Eva Gabor! In all professions, we are first judged by our appearance. If you dress like a successful home manager, you will be treated like one. Staying in a nightgown or pajamas doesn't make housework a dream. Even if you plan to shower after the heavier work is done, get dressed to greet your family. They will think you're a pro at whatever you do.

Dress for the job—aprons or orchids? Mechanics wear coveralls; artists wear smocks; gardeners wear grubbies. But a home manager doesn't have to look like a ragged cleaning lady or a mop-and-broom man all day, every day. Wear an apron when you're washing dishes and cooking. Wear jeans and a T-shirt when you vacuum. But when you've finished that grubby job, get into clothes that make you look and feel successful.

Work quickly. When I was first married, I worked in a clothing factory sewing front pockets into boys' corduroy pants for $1.25 an hour. When we reached the minimum standard of production, we were paid by the piece. The standard they set for me sounded impossible—it was less than a penny a pair. After my training probation, I was sewing only 240 pockets a day. I had met the limits set by my expectation.

This was the most boring work I've ever done. To break the monotony, I calculated how fast I would have to sew each piece to reach standard. I began setting time goals. "Today I will try to sew two dozen in a half-hour, which means one pocket every 75 seconds." Each day I cut my time a little. Within five months, I had increased my production far enough above standard so that I was sewing thousands of pockets every day and making half again my regular salary.

This principle can be applied at home. Did you know that an entire batch of diapers can be folded in five minutes, or that the dishwasher can be unloaded during a commercial break? If you learn to work faster, you can improve your home business. Use a timer to beat the clock for routine duties. Working quickly can become your habit. Pretend you're paying yourself. I expect the freezer-repair person, who charges $17 for the first 15 minutes, to really hustle. What would you expect of yourself if you were being paid for this project?

One last word of advice comes from a man who wrote to Ann Landers after taking over the housework for ten days. "Don't turn on the TV, it turns the iron in your blood to lead in your bottom."

Bunch as much as possible. It takes a certain block of time to set up and another to clean up. Get as much out of one mess as you can. Whenever I make bread, I mix a cake or a batch of cookies and still have only one bowl to wash. Preparing two lasagna casseroles takes only a few minutes longer than preparing one. But there is an art to knowing how much work to start. If I try to bake two batches of bread, mix a cake, and make cookies, the mess is still there when my energy is gone.

Avoid interruptions. It takes time after each interruption to start up and build momentum again. Expect *some* interruptions, especially with young children, but keep them to a minimum. When interrupted, ask yourself who caused it. Was it self-imposed? Was it necessary? If it happens often, ask if this type of interruption can be avoided. Finishing the basic morning routine can curb many an intrusion because you won't have to stop as often for such things as putting on socks and shoes or sweeping up cornflakes. A vital management technique stressed upon business executives is to do one thing at a time and finish it. When an interruption occurs at home, go back to the partially finished job before going on to another.

The telephone is a major interrupter. Answer calls, but keep them brief during heavy working hours. If you were in a nine to five job, you couldn't accept a forty-five-minute phone call from a friend. You can't when you are at work either, unless it is a *true* emergency. *(Remember:* phone-aholics have a crisis every day. The telephone is a wonderful invention. It helps keep friendships alive and saves hours of shopping and working on service projects, but it can gobble up work time. You are the manager; get control.) If you can polish the refrigerator or clean out a drawer while talking on the phone, fine, but count it as recreation, not efficient work time.

When the phone rings and it is a friend who wants to chat, ask if you can call back when you are not busy. Use the same courtesy and judgment in making *your* calls. Your light workday may be someone else's heavy workday. After identifying yourself, state the purpose of your call and ask if they have time to discuss it with you. Offer to call back later if necessary.

Have a quitting time. Housework is something that is never finished unless you set a quitting time for housekeeping duties. Set deadlines, both long-term and short. The Chinese prepare for the New Year by returning everything borrowed, paying off all debts, cleaning the house, and obtaining a spiritual renewal—it is their deadline. Your goal might be to finish spring cleaning by April or to have everything straightened and everyone clean by Saturday night. Use your calendar to help set realistic goals. Inviting guests into your home is an incentive to get every room in the house completely clean (or at least straightened up) at the same time. Don't make this a drudgery by insisting that the house be newly painted or that the new sofa be delivered before entertaining. When the goal is met, it is good to bask in that caught-up feeling.

Set short-term deadlines or goals throughout the day and use them as your guide. Edwin Bliss said, "When you think in terms of the task, instead of in terms of the time available for it, the sin of perfection sets in." He goes on to say that striving for excellence is healthy, but perfectionism is a waste of time. If I had to stay in the kitchen after dinner until it was perfectly clean, I would still be there at breakfast. Instead, we all work together for thirty minutes, getting as much done as possible, and then go on to other things.

Set long- and short-term time goals and then, if you don't get finished, evaluate whether to extend the time allotment or pack up and quit. It may be better in the long run to stop cleaning the closet, fix dinner and go back to it later than to face the results of dinner being two hours late.

Practical Application:

Call together all those who live with you and talk about the purposes for each room and what behavior will be permitted there. Write out your daily and weekly cleaning specifications for each room and post them in the closets.

Pick out one or two concepts of good work habits and concentrate on improving them for several weeks, and then work on another good habit.

✳ THREE ✳

Inner Space

*8
Less Is More

In our community, there is a woman who in recent years has had four cases filed against her by the district attorney for failure to maintain her premises. She accumulates "treasures" from her neighbors' trash bins. The second half of her duplex has been posted unsafe for human habitation because it was filled with debris. In her house, only a narrow path winds between the mountains of empty cans, bottles, papers, clothes, pots, and food scraps. She feels there is a use for everything she finds. She was billed $2,000 by the city last year to pay for the cleanup of her property. Twenty-six truckloads were hauled to the dump, taking 300 work hours. The sad thing is that her house and property are already overflowing again. She asks, "What is wrong with being in the salvage business? It has made millionaires of many people." This isn't salvage. Her compulsive collecting has made her property unusable. It drives away friends and turns neighbors into enemies.

All of us have the same problem in varying degrees. We keep things without knowing why or how to stop. We tuck it here, stash it there, stack and crowd until the house is impossible to clean. With every payday, sale, birthday, and holiday, we crowd in more—and overcrowding breeds clutter. You have four options to ease this situation: throw it out, change your shelving habits, buy more space, or move away. People often try to solve the problem in reverse by first buying new space. But the new space quickly becomes as cluttered as the old if habits aren't improved. Eventually you will run out of places to put new shelves and chests and the money to buy them. The following hints can help you start at the beginning and build enough self-discipline to say good-bye to your loot.

SEVEN WAYS TO THROW IT OUT

1. ***Count the cost.*** Storage space costs money. What would you put on a shelf which cost $5 a year to rent? Not your ninth-grade textbook. What about the Bingo game with twelve missing numbers? If it won't pay its own rent, throw it out. My dentist learned this lesson after many miserable years. "It costs $850 a year to rent the space for this crowded laboratory," he said. "One whole cupboard is taken up by brass denture molds I've never used in five years. And the dentist who had them previously hadn't used them in seven years. Look at how much it's costing me to keep them."

2. ***Ask yourself these questions:*** When will I use it? Did I use it last year? Is it a treasure? Can I get these supplies again, easily (sawdust for pin cushions)? Is this item often seen at garage sales? Could I buy used baby furniture, if there is a next time, rather than store mine? Is this an unfinished project that I'll never finish? Is it safe? (Even if it's valuable, you may be risking all your other possessions. I'll save newspapers and magazines for two months if the Boy Scouts will come and haul them away, but no longer. Get rid of old medicine, too.)

3. ***Cut down and eliminate duplication.*** Ten years pass quickly. In that time, you could be given a waffle iron, coffee pot, donut maker, crock pot, bread mixer, automatic vegetable cutter, four-slice toaster, crepe pan, deep fryer, blender, microwave oven, noodle maker, and broiler. Where can you possibly store them? On the counter? Luckily, some of them will break. Use dual-purpose appliances wherever possible (and don't forget how many things a stove can do). If a donut maker will be used only on Halloween, why not use just a saucepan. Take a look around your house. Try living with just four pans.

Trying to merge households temporarily or permanently can multiply your housekeeping problems if you don't take control and make decisions. Which of the two electric mixers and eight mixing bowls shall we keep in the cupboard? In a permanent merger such as marriage or inheriting your grandmother's household, you might decide to get rid of part of it. If the merger is tentative—a divorcée moving in with parents or singles teaming up as roommates—store the unnecessary items, cutting back until you fit comfortably into the new space.

Throwing it out includes selling it or giving it to a lucky friend or in-law. Remember, less is more. Look in the closet. How many types of furniture polish are there? Get rid of those you're not using or don't like. Just because you paid money for something doesn't obligate you to use it all. (You may have paid $1.25 for the leaf polish which is only half gone, but it killed every plant you used it on.) When I was examining my laundry supplies, I found samples of dry bleach and soap that I hadn't tried in two years. The plumber's pipe goop, left when the house was built nine years ago, was still there. There were two brands of enzyme presoak and three types of fabric softener. I vowed to keep only one brand of each product and use up the others within two weeks. I cleared out a whole shelf.

4. *Set limits.* How many aluminum pie tins do you really use? Six to bake round bread and a few for taking to parties when you want to skip the bother of having the pan returned—twelve should be enough. Send them to school for the kindergarten class. And dump all those extra paper sacks, cottage-cheese cartons, and butter tubs. Get rid of the plastic refrigerator containers and use a few glass jars. You will save space; and because you can see the contents, you will use up the leftovers before they spoil. Set aside a corner or box for fabric or craft scraps. When it is full, that's the limit. Don't collect more. I figure if I give my scraps to someone who has the time to use them now, when I reach a slower time in life and want to piece quilts, some young busy mother will give me hers. Set limits for clothing, too. We wear the ones we like 80 percent of the time. Why keep all the others?

If you have trouble throwing things out, your children will probably develop the same bad habit. Unless you set limits, the children's belongings seem to grow right along with them until there is enough to fill a house of their own. Every Christmas and birthday they get another hobby or collection. In ten years, they will each have twenty large boxes saved in the closet unless you produce a younger sister or brother to quickly destroy them. You must set the example by setting limits on what can be saved and what must be thrown out.

5. *Move.* Moving tends to expose every item of the household and create a time of accelerated elimination. A family that doesn't move often may try the pretend method: pretend you're moving, but

tackle one room at a time. Hold a big garage sale. Let someone else tuck it, stash it, and crowd it.

Parents who are not involved in many moves tend to settle in, filling each room as a child vacates, lining the walls with chests and shelves and stuffing the basement and attic with past hobbies and clothes. As one woman watched an older couple next door move, she counted eighteen beds—true story.

6. **Push back those pangs of parting.** Two weeks after you have given away all your old sweaters, you'll find you could have ripped them out to make beautiful afghans. Don't let this kind of experience stop you. The painful decision to throw something out makes such an impression that you recall things you've parted with better than those you've stored. If you hadn't given it away, you probably wouldn't have remembered you had it.

7. **Stabilize.** After your home has reached optimum capacity, with the cupboards and closets full but clutter still at a minimum, the trick is to equalize the incoming with the outgoing—and that doesn't mean outgoing to the garage. Some garages are used for cars, some for workshops, but most are "halfway-out" spots. When my family itemized after a garage fire, we realized that most of what was destroyed was worthless junk we just hadn't parted with. Now we have limits on garage storage: holiday decorations, garden supplies, tools, and the car. When we feel the squeeze in the house, the castouts have to go to charity, not the garage. If you get a new robe, don't save the old one until the new one is worn out; pass it on. What about last year's coat? The old iron?

By cutting down on excess and making a place for those things you decide to keep, you will find a new freedom: more space without paying for it! It's easier to keep clean. It's easier to find things. It's more time for you.

FOUR WAYS TO PUT AN END TO ODDS AND ENDS

1. **Find a place for everything.** Start now by finding a place for each additional item you bring into the home, including this book. No more halfway spots. The only time you are justified in leaving something out is if it is intended to be a decoration. Then begin noticing the types of things that cause the most clutter: toys, clothing, mail. Do they have a place? If not, create one.

Clutter is a typical problem in our society because it's not unusual for a home in the United States to have 300,000 items! Making a place for everything is essential when you stop to consider that only six items left out of place in a room can make it look messy. A concentrated effect to find a "home" for each object will be rewarded.

When you purchase furniture or add shelves, you should be drawn toward storage features. A single adult may be able to create a place for everything in two weeks, but it may take a family a whole year. Make your plan and follow it.

2. *Create a pile-it corner.* We have a pile-it corner in our kitchen (out of view) that is not used for food preparation. It is a fifteen-minute parking zone. Here we put school papers, notices, permission slips, and other projects that come and go quickly. Library books and other borrowed items will be put there so they don't get lost in our belongings. (We also have a stash-it drawer in almost every room.)

3. *Have a place for storage.* Our dentist has an effective method—he keeps an active file for those patients who come in regularly and an inactive file for those who haven't been in for more than a year. This saves the secretary time and effort. This principle works at home, too. Seldom-used items shouldn't be using prime space. Put them in an inactive area, but cover and *label* them first. Be careful not to store things like books, linens, or leather goods in a moist basement, or bottled or canned food in a hot attic.

4. *Put things away while they're still in hand.* Are you affected with dropsy? That's the habit of setting things down before they are where they belong. The energy you spend making a place for everything will be wasted if you don't get things there. It takes more time to come back later to put things away. Why set the potting soil by the stairs to go to the garage and then leave it there for three days? Halfway spots add to the clutter of your home. A person who leaves an article out automatically flashes on the reason for its being there. The uninvolved observer only sees it out of place. That is why a mother will call a child back to put away his coat and not be concerned with her coat because she is going out again in fifteen minutes. If you stand at the door and look at things through a visitor's eyes, you can spot collection centers.

At work or at home, we leave things out as reminders. "I'll leave this letter out so I will remember to answer it soon." "If I leave the onion sets here on the counter, I'll be reminded to plant them." Do you write? Did you plant? The advantage of an effective Running Project List (see page 13) is that you can put something away and not worry about forgetting it. If you're one of those people who just puts things off, put it on a list and at least get the item out of sight.

HOW TO SET UP A HOME FILING SYSTEM THAT WORKS

Every home needs to have a system for filing personal records. No matter how modest your home facilities may be, you need a special place to keep tax records, legal items, insurance policies, and the like. Beyond that, you may have business, school, church; or career-related articles and stories you want to keep and be able to find.

The equipment you need doesn't have to be elaborate. A metal file cabinet is nice, but an accordion folder or a sturdy box will do just as well. The important thing is to organize everything under *one* system— and I recommend keeping it as simple as possible. It doesn't matter who organizes your home filing system, but use the talents of the one with the best business sense.

A brochure put out by the United States Department of Agriculture entitled "Keeping Family/Household Records; What to Discard," recommends that important, hard-to-replace papers such as birth and marriage certificates, stocks, and bonds be kept in a safe-deposit box; that the necessary financial papers such as receipts, unpaid bills, and canceled checks be put in an active file, and that after three years, the papers from the active file be moved to dead storage. This is all a way of categorizing *first*, before you embark on the actual filing. Following is a chart adapted from U.S.D.A. Brochure #638F:

Many home managers neglect to compile a household inventory to be put in their safe deposit box. If there is a fire or burglary in your home, this record will help you remember what has to be replaced and how much each item was worth. An inventory also may show that you need to increase your insurance because your possessions are worth more than you thought. The best way to go about compiling a household inventory is to start with a sheet of paper for each room in the house or apartment. Start at one point in the room and go all the way around, listing *everything*. Don't forget cameras, watches, bicy-

HOME FILING CHECKLIST

Safe Deposit Box
1. birth certificates
2. citizenship papers
3. marriage certificates
4. adoption papers
5. divorce decrees
6. wills
7. death certificates
8. deeds
9. titles to automobiles
10. household inventory
11. veteran's papers
12. bonds and stock certificates
13. important contracts

Active File
1. tax receipts
2. unpaid bills
3. paid-bill receipts
4. current bank statements
5. current canceled checks
6. income tax working papers
7. employment records
8. health benefit information
9. credit card information (with account numbers)
10. insurance policies
11. copies of wills
12. family health records
13. appliance manuals and warranties
14. receipts of items under warranty
15. education information
16. inventory of safe-deposit box (and key)
17. loan statements
18. loan payment books
19. receipts of expensive items not yet paid for
20. memberships, licenses requiring yearly renewal (such as dog licenses)

Dead Storage
all active file papers over three years old

Items to Discard
1. salary statements (after checking on W-2 form)
2. canceled checks for cash or nondeductible expenses
3. expired warranties
4. Coupons after expiration date
5. other records no longer needed

cles, tools, slide and movie projectors, car, TVs, and stereos. For each item, list what it is, how much it cost, when it was purchased, the model number, brand name, and a general description. Taking pictures of the rooms and your household possessions will make identification or replacement easier. Arrange expensive collections, silver, and jewelry separately and take closeup pictures.

The business filing technique most adaptable to the home is the subject filing system with an index. For most homes, just the subject system alone is adequate. For the subject system, a key word or phrase like "unpaid bills," "guarantees," or "Halloween" is written on the tab of the file folder, and all the papers or ideas dealing with that subject are put in that folder. Start with the twenty suggested categories for an active financial file as suggested on the government list and see how it works for you. You can put fifty to seventy-five papers in a folder before it needs to be divided.

The advantages of this system are that it has unlimited expansion possibilities, and it automatically groups records or articles on the same subject together. The disadvantage is that there is sometimes indecision about where to put things. For instance, should you want to file the article, "The First 12 Days of School," will it go behind "school," "money," or the "author," Erma Bombeck. In a few months, you may not remember which subject you filled it under and have to hunt for the article. If you have more than fifty file folders, you'll probably need to use a cross-reference index with your filing system, which will also solve the problem just mentioned of the lost article.

To start a filing system at home, Joyce and Jerry divided their papers into four major categories: (1) important active financial papers, (2) general articles and stories, (3) art, craft, and sewing instructions, and (4) genealogical records (tracing your family roots). The art, craft, and sewing ideas were filed in a box in the sewing room, and the other three categories were each given a separate drawer in the file cabinet. This way, Grandma Lucy's life history wasn't mixed in with macramé directions or insurance policies. Each of the major categories was then divided into various subtopics (see the following list) and a file folder was started for each subtopic. (Not every home will need as many or even the same categories as Jerry and Joyce).

1. *active financial:* tax receipts, employment records, insurance policies, bank statements, etc. (see Active File list, page 65)

2. *general:* mother, Thanksgiving, garden, maps, puppet plays, Old Testament stories, etc.
3. *art, craft, sewing:* interior decorating ideas, furniture refinishing, paper flowers, stuffed animals and dolls, upholstery techniques, drapery instructions, etc.
4. *genealogy:* (divided by family names) Almire, Thompson, Browne, etc.

Joyce and Jerry used the simple-subject filing system to file the material behind each of the separate categories. Because they had so much material in the general file, they found it helpful to cross-index it. As each article was slipped behind a subject, they wrote it down on a 4 x 6 index card, indicating on the right side which subject it was filed under. If there was a possibility of it going under another subject, title, or author, they made another card. All of these cards were kept in alphabetical order in a little metal index box. More than one entry was made on a card.

How to use an index card system to organize your home filing system.

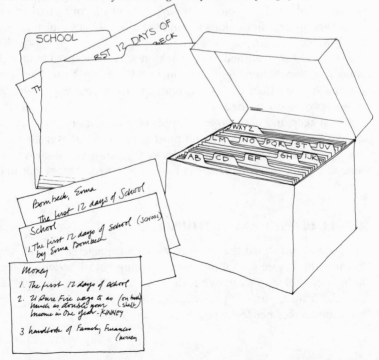

Before you get too far into filing, consider your needs. When Jerry and Joyce started to organize their filing system, they had huge piles of old canceled checks and receipts, and magazines with "good" articles and stories. They put all these things they had collected, along with their filing cabinet, folders, and stack of index cards, into a spare bedroom and worked on it whenever they had a chance. But they were unsure of what must be kept for tax purposes, and the new magazines arrived faster than they could go through the old ones. Finally they decided to take a clean-sweep approach with the magazines. If they hadn't needed those articles in the last ten years, chances are they wouldn't be needing them in the future, so they got rid of most of the original stack and started anew.

They found that it wasn't necessary to keep everything for tax purposes. Jerry and Joyce discarded old checks and bills that didn't directly relate to an entry on their tax return. (Keep all medical bills for three years to back up your canceled checks.) After the salary statements were checked against the annual W-2 form, they threw them away. Though the Internal Revenue Service has three years in which to audit federal income tax returns, beware: in "unusual cases," the government has six years to collect the tax or to start legal proceedings if you failed to report more than 25 percent of your gross income. There are no time limitations if you filed a fraudulent return or if you failed to file a return.

Jerry and Joyce learned to cut back on what they saved, and if they wanted it, they filed it right away instead of saving it up. They threw out much more than they kept, realizing from past experience how little they actually needed.

If you keep and need large amounts of information, you may need a more detailed filing system, but most homes can put everything they will ever need to keep in two file drawers. Even if you don't yet have time to organize your papers into folders, get them all together in one place.

A FULL CLOSET AND NOTHING TO WEAR

We have all witnessed the scene in which a teenage girl spends forty-five minutes before school pulling everything out of her closet, trying to find something to wear. What she is doing is flipping through "mistakes," "dislike," and "unmatchables" to find something that looks good and makes her feel well dressed.

Unfortunately, most of us have not progressed beyond this "teen-age" problem, except that we go through the process in less time. We wear 20 percent of our clothes 80 percent of the time. The secret is to award a prime area in the closet for the favorite few.

Set aside a block of time—perhaps an hour on Saturday morning—to go through your closet. Make a distinction between clothes and shoes you wear often and those you seldom wear. Ask yourself, *"Why* don't I wear it?" If it's too small, you don't like it, it doesn't fit, it's the wrong color for you, or it's out of style, put it in one pile on the floor or bed (of course you made your bed before you started!). If it doesn't match any of your other clothes or needs mending or cleaning, put it in a second pile—the "maybe" pile. If it's something you wear every day or every week, place it in a third pile. One college woman who cleaned out her closets using this system said she asked herself only one question: "Have I worn it in the last year?" If not, out it went. No debate.

Put back in the closet only those clothes that are proven good friends—no maybes. Never put an item in the closet unless it's ready to wear—clean, pressed, and mended. Organize by separating suits, shirts, slacks, and sweaters, or by hanging matchables together (this will simplify the dressing procedure).

What about the others? A few more decisions are necessary. The clothing that will be among the friends but needs care (cleaning or mending) should be in a separate pile to be taken care of. To get these items back in shape, set aside a time for mending or for dropping them off at the cleaners. If a garment needs a matchmate, belt, or tie, write it on your shopping list or want list. These garments should also be laundered, pressed, and mended so they'll be ready when you want them.

Some clothing you are ready to part with now. Put it in a bag for the local thrift shop, the Salvation Army, or Good Will before the mood passes. One woman met her neighbor at the fabric store. "I hate everything I own," she said, "so I set it all out on the porch for the Veterans to pick up. All I have is what I'm wearing." Not many of us can do that—but then maybe we would be better off having three outfits we like than a closet full of "obligations."

A spare closet would be ideal for out-of-season or out-of-fit clothing to keep it from wrinkling. If you don't have a spare closet, a cedar chest, trunk, suitcase, or even a box with a lid will do for storage. Another possibility is to hang the less desirable garments (those you are not ready to part with on one side of your closet and cover them with a blanket to get them out of sight. Gradually you'll get rid of these "strangers."

At college, when we had only three feet of closet space, most of the women had to get up early to press what they intended to wear for the day. There would have been plenty of room for a week's wardrobe if

How to create more closet space. On the left, before; on the right, after.

they had simplified by putting their out-of-season clothing in the communal storage cage instead of dressing from the ironing board.

It takes courage to get rid of clothing that doesn't fit. For some, doing so means defeat: "If I give away these clothes, I have given up hope of ever losing weight." Take another view: "I haven't been able to wear these in the last two years; they are out of style. I'll give them

away, lose weight, and reward myself with a new wardrobe." Keep hope and get rid of unwearable clothes. (And don't feel obligated to wear out someone else's castoffs, either.)

I get a kick out of going to a high-school play and seeing the "costumes" that came from Mom and Dad's teen days. Saving clothing that "might be needed someday" is a luxury that most of us don't have room to indulge in. Clothes get worse with age, so pass them on. Let someone else save the "costumes."

Now that your closet contains only clothing that is ready for wear and proven friendly, consider making more room in your closet by improving its physical features. First think about perking it up with a fresh coat of paint or some lively wallpaper or contact paper. If you own your own home, you might make plans for permanent alterations in the closet structure. Those who live in apartments or who move often can use movable accessories to add space.

A second rod hung with chain or ropes in half the closet for the shorter items can give you 25 percent more rod space. Step shelves (see Chapter 10, How to Create More Space) stacked at the end of a closet will give space for shoes and other accessories. A small wooden or cardboard chest with drawers or even a narrow bookcase can be set at the end of the closet or under the shorter clothing. A towel rod can be used for belts and ties or slacks. Even a stack of vegetable bins could be used for sweaters or shoes. A long board set on bricks on top of the permanent closet shelf would give a second shelf above the rod.

Get control of your closet. Enjoy the lovely feeling of going to the closet, quickly selecting an outfit, and putting it on. It's a good way to start a day.

Practical Application:

Remember your past mistakes. When buying new clothing, plan carefully instead of purchasing on impulse, and don't buy too many clothes in one season.

Set a time twice a year to go through your closet to separate "friends" from "strangers." Get the friends ready to wear, eliminate what you can, and make a storage place for the others. Evaluate ways to make more efficient use of shelves and of the space below clothing and at the ends of a closet.

*9
Cupboards and Closets

Do you need more room? In the process of everyday living, even an orderly, neat cupboard becomes cluttered and jumbled and bulges with the forgotten. There is a solution: accept the fact that cupboards and closets must be cleaned at least once a year, and more often in areas of frequent use. Having neat cupboards and closets not only saves work time but also offers more actual storage space. Try applying the following rules as you do your cleaning to create extra storage space that is safe and convenient.

STORAGE HABITS

Keep everything within reach of the area where the work is to be done. This is especially important in the kitchen. Potatoes should be near the sink where they will be peeled, pot holders should be near the stove, and a pencil should be by the phone. Gravy boats and serving dishes don't have to be stored with the dinnerware just because they match. Keep them by the stove where they will be filled with hot vegetables or near the sink where the salad is prepared. Store items where their use begins—bed sheets in the bedroom; a glass and spoon with the medicine; towels, toilet tissue, and hot-water bottles in the bathroom. By storing cleanser, brooms, and paper towels in several locations, you will save many steps.

Make everything earn its place. Items used most often should be stored between waist and eye level. Infrequently used items, covered and labeled, should be stored in inactive storage areas away from your busy kitchen. The turkey roasting pan and pressure canner alone take a whole cupboard if they are allowed.

Cupboard storage is determined by size, weight, breakability, shape, and use. The highest and lowest storage space is for seldom-used items, but keep the high-level storage simple. Large items like cake or pie covers are best stored above because they can be lifted down in one movement. Small items are best stored below because they can be dangerous and difficult to handle when stacked above eye level. Store bottles, cans, and jars at eye level so they can be easily seen and reached, leaving the shorter containers toward the front. Always put items back in the same spot, even if other family members don't. (It may help to put labels on the front edge of the shelf.)

Is it safe? Household detergents are now the number-one cause of poisoning among children age five and under. (Plants are number two.) Plant food, pesticides, medicines, and matches must be stored up high and locked. Even if you don't have young children, think of the rest of us with curious toddlers who may drop by for a visit. Keep knives in a rack, out of drawers. Keep paint and other flammable materials away from the flames of the fireplace, water heater, or furnace.

Accessories can improve space: step-shelves, half-shelves, racks, files, turntables, bins, boxes, dishpans, vertical dividers, and drawer dividers. These don't necessarily have to cost money. (See Chapter 10, How to Create More Space). Carefully consider whether the accessory is really helpful. Don't put six goblets on a turntable when twelve goblets would fit on the shelf without it. Look at your storage areas with imagination. Sheets and towels can be set vertically on a shelf just like books in a case for easy selection. A shoe box or bread pan could hold up plastic lids or packets of seasoning mixes and flavored drinks.

Consider anything to be permanently attached if you use nails or screws. Big holes left in the walls and woodwork reduce the value of your home or apartment. Take pity on the next dwellers—before hanging anything on the wall, be it pictures, dispensers, racks, or rods, make a paper pattern the exact size and shape of it. Tape or pin the pattern to the wall and rearrange until you find just the right spacing before attaching it.

Unless it is pretty, keep it out of sight. Put away as much of your stuff as possible. Even open shelves are hard to keep looking neat and tidy, but those things that must be left out can be pleasing to the eye if they are balanced in a logical arrangement. The more counter space you have, the more you can set on it before it looks cluttered. This is a paradox, because it is the home with limited counter space that doesn't have enough cupboards.

A KITCHEN OF CONVENIENCE

Are you working harder than you need to in the kitchen? If you're like me, the kitchen is where most of your work is done. Let's stop and look at your kitchen. The things you do in your kitchen may not be the same as the things I do in mine, but there are many similarities. We can look at your movement patterns and organize your kitchen so that you can get your work done easier and faster. This is one place where an investment of time now can pay off in dividends of more time later on.

Let's start with something fun—a cake. What do you need? Where do you mix it? In what will you bake it? First, you reach for the bowl. If you have good storage habits, the bowl will be within easy reach. *Stop!* Where is the most convenient spot in your kitchen to place the bowl for mixing this cake? The best place probably already has something on it because it is your "prime" area. Clear it off. If this is the perfect mixing area, you need utensils, ingredients, and an electric outlet within reach. The most workable mixing centers are on a counter between the sink and the stove. Are you going to mix by hand or zip it up with a mixer? How many steps did it take to pick up the whisk or hand mixer, and were any of those steps wasted? If it took three steps to reach your present storage area when it could have been stored only two steps away, you are working 30 percent harder than you need to. You may say, "What is one step?" Multiply it by the number of times you reach for something, and it could be as much as the length of two football fields. Who would walk that far for a spoon?

Now for the cake. If you prefer the simplicity of the package mix, keep it in this mixing center where you are ready to whip it up. What if we make a cake from scratch? Stand in front of your bowl. Are the sugar and flour within reach? And are they together? Count the steps you took to get them. If it's necessary, choose a more convenient place for them within reach of your mixing center. Perhaps the flour and sugar containers are too large for this working area. A colorful canister set to hold a smaller quantity might work better. If you enjoy cooking great creations, trying new recipes, or baking often, you could justify leaving your canisters on the counter top because of their frequent use. Put spices, flavorings, food colorings, and levenings within easy reach in this mixing center by using a step-shelf, rack, or turntable.

Now that the cake is mixed and ready to bake, what will you bake it in? If the cake pan is behind the toaster and under the waffle iron at the other end of the kitchen, you will need to find a closer storage spot. Cooking and baking can become dreaded chores when you can't find anything. You can now set up your kitchen logically and make it fit your cooking needs. After one young mother had gone to all the trouble of setting up her mixing center in a corner, she didn't use it because it was more natural to turn around and face the open portion of the house. Watching the children while she worked was a more important need, and the mixing area had to be moved to meet this need.

Don't be fooled into thinking that just because you know where everything is in your kitchen, it is convenient. You will have to stop and look for habit patterns that are not efficient. Marilyn pinpointed her self-defeating habits by hauling everything in the kitchen out to the porch. Every time she needed something, she went out and got it and then put it away near the place it was used. After two weeks, more than half the kitchen equipment was still on the porch, exposing her true needs. She put the seasonal equipment such as canning supplies in the storage area and gave away the never-used utensils, appliances, and dishes. The special serving bowls and candy dishes were all put together in one cupboard with the good china. Marilyn created convenient work centers in the closed-in cupboards and used the outer cupboards for less-frequently used items. She now has the step-saving advantages of a small kitchen and the inner space of a large kitchen. With her kitchen rearranged, it was easier to keep clean and tidy, and Marilyn was rid of free-loaders. If you tried Marilyn's experiment, which items would find their way back into your kitchen in a week?

We have already set up one kitchen center—for mixing—but we will need to design three more specific work areas for our efficient kitchen. The cooking center will naturally be centered around the stove. Think through the movements for making your favorite meal. Is everything you need within arm's reach? Head off the natural tendency to include the garlic, onion, and chili powders with the sweet spices, because you need them near the range. The stove should have its own set of salt and pepper shakers. I store the wooden spoons, spatula, and tongs in a container near the stove top, since my kitchen drawers are too far from my cooking center. Notice your movements as you get a pan. If the pans are to be stored where they will be used, they would go in a cupboard next to the stove; but if you normally put water in the pan before setting it on the burner, maybe they should be kept in a cupboard near the sink.

For the most part, you need only as many pans as you have burners. Trying Marilyn's experiment with your pans, pick out four versatile pans and put the others in a big box far enough away so that it is a noticeable effort to get them. Go for another pan only when you absolutely need it. Wouldn't it be less work simply to wash the pan soaking in the sink than to get another one from the box? You will have found that you can get by with fewer pans, and that your cupboards won't be as crowded. This same principle applies to mixing and serving bowls and knives. You can use only one knife at a time—two paring knives, a bread knife, and a chef's knife are enough to meet all my needs.

The third center, the sink, should have the towels and dishcloths nearby, in a drawer if possible or in a box on a shelf if drawer space is limited. Don't be afraid to try something different if it makes sense. You don't always have to have the silver in one drawer and the utensils in another just because your mother did it that way. Maybe it would be more convenient to keep the utensils nearer the mixing center in a plastic dishpan or ice-cream bucket. If you have a shallow drawer in the right spot, try using it for the spices, laying them on their sides so the labels are visible. Towels and dishcloths might be stored vertically in a drawer rather than stacked on top of each other.

The fourth and last area in your kitchen will be for the tableware. According to the place for eating and washing, what will be the best spot to store the dishes? How can you set up the dishwashing movements to get them as close to the "final resting place" as possible when finished? Work right to left or left to right, but try to store these dishes away from the other work centers. This tableware area will vary from kitchen to kitchen. In our home, everyday dishes and glasses are in the lower cabinets so the children can set the table and empty the dishwasher without adult assistance, an arrangement that saves me an hour a day.

Because of the safety needs or the physical nature of your kitchen, the "first-used" rule can be amended. Dry cereal boxes may fit only on a tall shelf, even if it's far from the table. The cookie sheets will have to go wherever they fit, sideways under the sink or in the stove drawer, rather than in the mixing center. For safety, you will want the dishwasher detergent to be up high rather than under the sink. Hang knives from a wall magnet or rack to keep them out of drawers and away from fingers.

"The efficiency challenge" is an interesting game I indulge in while looking through home and family magazines. When I see a picture of a kitchen, I ask, "Would I like to work in this kitchen? Where would I put the four work centers? Is this kitchen easy to clean?" I recognize the importance of atmosphere and decor, and I also know that there are a few cooks who don't make 10 loaves of bread, 2 cakes, and 108 cookies every week, but some interior decorators give too little thought to practicality. For instance, an ad emphasizing easy-care, no-wax floors had a four-foot swag crystal chandelier in the kitchen (not dining room). Another kitchen, designed for a gourmet cook, had moss rock walls behind the counters—ought to be fun cleaning off grease splatters or whipped cream. One magazine spotlighted a lovely old-fashioned kitchen with the flour and sugar canisters on the fourth shelf above the work counter and the paper towels ten steps from the sink and stove, on the backside of an island. You have probably already guessed the types of things that drive me wild—lots of open shelves, hanging pots and pans that you can't reach unless you are seven feet tall, every utensil in the house sitting in a bucket on the counter or hanging from the wall, and plants sitting in the middle of a work center. I just hate to do extra work.

It probably isn't wise to challenge a friend's or your mother's kitchen for efficiency, but try it on a magazine—your ideas won't hurt their feelings. Use their pictures and imagine various work processes, and you'll better understand your needs and preferences. Then, as you hunt for a new apartment, buy a home, or remodel the one you have, you can fill your kitchen needs.

An efficient kitchen has enough equipment to perform the necessary jobs, but not so much that the cleanup is difficult. You may find two sets of tableware are necessary to save turning on the dishwasher before it's full, but you don't want too many dishes, either. My father-in-law tells of the winter he and another bachelor spent eighteen hours washing the five hundred dishes the two of them had accumulated, one meal at a time. They cooked in a kitchen equipped to serve meals to huge forest-fire crews, and they had unwisely put off doing the dishes. Learning from past experience, they kept out only two pans and two place settings of dishes and locked away all the others.

Following is a skeleton list of kitchen equipment. As in all areas of home management, you will want to make it fit your needs and circumstances.

wire whip	measuring spoons	waste basket
hand mixer	1 small mixing bowl	1 paring knife
1 small saucepan	1 large mixing bowl	1 serrated-edge knife
1 medium saucepan	sieve	1 butcher knife
1 fry pan	grater	bread board
pressure cooker	peeler	rolling pin
1 9 x 13 cake pan	cookie sheet	1 small casserole
long wooden spoon	cooling racks	dish with lid
pancake turner	2 bread pans	1 large casserole
rubber spatula	2 plastic dishpans	dish with lid
measuring cups		

Practical Application:

Plan your kitchen by defining the four work centers and by tracing your work patterns. Select only the necessary pans, bowls, and utensils from your kitchen equipment and logically put them where they can be reached and where they will be first used. Check to see if you are still using the proper shelving habits. You are well on your way to having an efficient kitchen with organized cupboards and closets.

✳10
How to Create More Space

If you have gotten rid of all the excess and have made the best use of storage space but still need more room, you may find your answer in the following suggestions. A wide array of ready-made space extenders is available in stores and catalogs, but the following are generally much less expensive and are easy to make. Besides these ideas, watch magazines, newspapers, and books for other ways to create new space. Caution: any open shelf with exposed contents is harder to keep looking tidy than a shelf behind doors. An open shelf requires more cleaning and straightening and can't hold as much without looking crowded. If you're thinking of building open shelves, stop to consider how this effort to create more space will look in a year.

STEP-SHELVES

When Margaret set out to make a place for everything and took a critical look at her cupboards, she found a recurring "stacking" problem. "Because my silverware box is only five inches high," explained Margaret, "and I didn't want to waste space above it, I stacked the trays and platters on top of it. Every time we needed silver, I lifted down all the trays and took out the chest. For neatness, I had to put them all away again before company arrived. After the silverware was washed, I had to go through the whole packing process again. When my children helped, they weren't as careful as I, and the cupboard doors got scratched and dented."

Margaret's objective became to reach each item in one motion, and so she invented step-shelves. A step-shelf is a shelf with legs that is not attached to the cupboard. It can be the same width as the original shelf or it can be shorter and not as deep.

Margaret went through each cupboard looking for unused "head

Step-shelf.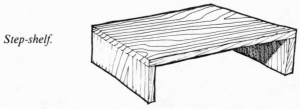

space" and stacks. For instance, there were 12 inches of unused space above the silverware chest. By making a step-shelf to fit over the chest, she could store the toaster on top of it. To make the step-shelf, Margaret measured the desired height and width. Allowing 1 inch above the chest, she cut two narrow boards for the legs, 6 inches high and 12 inches long—the depth of the cupboard. The base was to be 20 inches long and 12 inches wide. After gluing the legs to the bottom of the base and painting it all (contact paper works well, too) she set it in the cupboard.

In another cupboard, Margaret found 5 inches of lost space above the drinking glasses. By making a step-shelf to set over the glasses, a layer of cups could be put on top, doubling the usable shelf space. In a third cupboard, Margaret used vertical step-dividers to separate the baking tins, cookie sheets, and dough board. In a fourth cupboard, she created a second level for the pans so each pan and lid could be

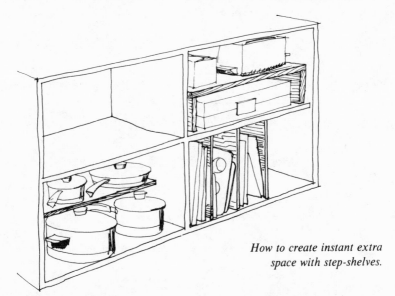

How to create instant extra space with step-shelves.

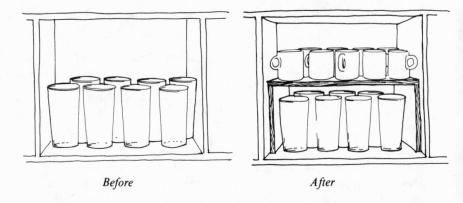

Before   *After*

stored together to save hunting, moving, and unstacking. Portable shelves were also put under the bathroom and kitchen sinks.

These step-shelves can be easily changed as circumstances vary because they are not permanently attached. And you don't have to be a carpenter to make them. Margaret used pressed wood to make her shelves and had it cut at the lumberyard, figuring on graph paper how to cut the large board to best advantage. If you would rather spend the money than use the time, similar units can be purchased commercially, but they may not fit the exact dimensions of your space.

Perhaps you have spotted wasted space above the spices. A step-shelf can help here, too, but it doesn't even have to be glued. Soup cans, boxes, or bricks could be used as spacers to hold up a narrow board at the back of the spice area.

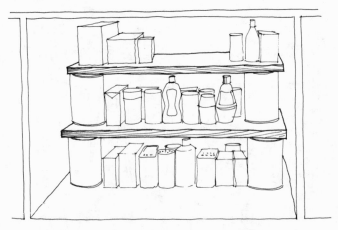

How to create more room in the spice area.

Several of these step-shelves stacked and glued together at the end of a closet will provide a place for books and games or hats and shoes. To make it easier for young children to hang up their clothes, lay a rod between two of these closet shelf units (see illustration below).

BOXES

Boxes can be used in hundreds of places to make better use of shelves and drawers. Covering them with contact paper is not only pleasing to the eye but also seems to give them more durability and keeps insects from hiding between the layers of paper.

How to use step-shelves to create more closet space.

1. Shoe boxes are good drawer dividers for socks, underwear, and pajamas, giving each type of clothing a specific territory. They are good for separating toys to keep them from becoming junk in the toy box. To prevent spilling if the box is dropped, make an elastic band by sewing a strip of elastic together, and snap it around the box to hold the lid on. Labeling the end of the box or drawing on a picture for the small child allows easy identification. The contents can be seen through clear plastic shoe boxes, but they aren't very durable.

2. We keep a 12″ x 8″ box (large enough to hold a baby book) for each child to keep his mementos and special pictures and certificates until they can be mounted. These books are shelved high enough to be out of the reach of little hands.

3. Cold-cereal boxes make terrific organizers for magazines.

4. Stand tall, narrow boxes on their sides in a cupboard to make a place for cookie sheets or trays.

5. Large vegetable and fruit boxes can serve as files or drawers on a shelf in any workroom.

6. Large, heavy boxes such as those that refrigerators or washing machines come in can be transformed into temporary closets by sliding a broom handle or pipe through the sides. Support the area under the rod holes with extra pieces of wood or cardboard. Put the rod at least 4 inches down from the top of the box and 14 inches out from the back to allow space for the hanger.

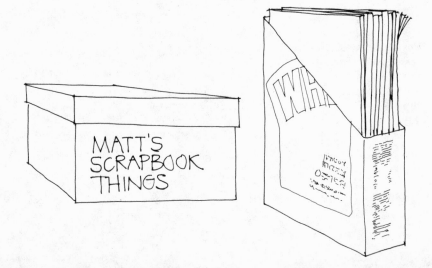

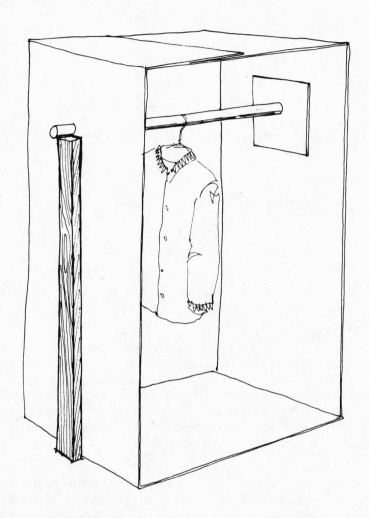

BASKETS AND BINS

Plastic dishpans and laundry baskets have the same endless possibilities as boxes. They are durable, easy to move and clean, and can help you separate and organize in almost any room. Whether they are under the bed or bathroom sink, small things can be effortlessly pulled out for your selection. When a craft or sewing project is interrupted, take a minute to gather the supplies into a plastic dishpan (just like tote trays in school), and they are all together when it's time to start again.

Baskets in the laundry room
can serve as dividers for wash loads.
As each household member brings soiled clothing
to the room, he sorts it into the appropriate basket.
When a basket is full, that batch is washed.

Going one step further, a drawer-filled cabinet can be created from dishpans or hard plastic storage bins available in many sizes from a school-supply house or an office- or restaurant-supply store. Two pairs of small wooden runners are nailed to the sides of the cabinet, leaving a space between the runners to hold the lip of each bin. The trick here is careful measurement to get the right size bin for your opening, but it's so much easier than making wooden drawers.

Plastic buckets from your local ice-cream stand or gallon-size cans from a cafeteria make great dividers for nails and small parts in the workshop. "If you can't find it, what's the use of having it?" says my father, a heating contractor. He has a whole wall of tilted shelves lined with labeled cans, dividing the many small parts he needs in his business.

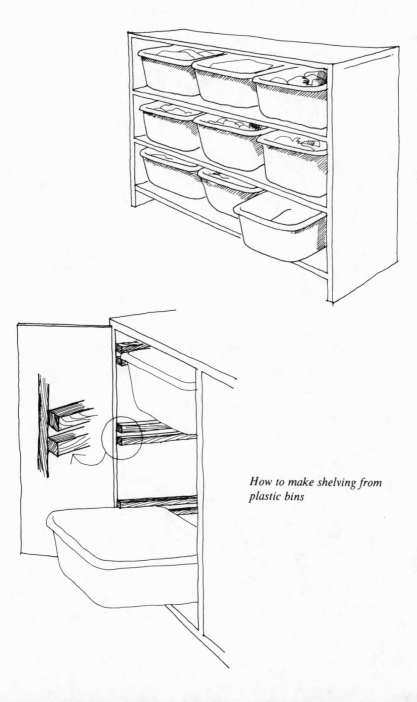

*How to make shelving from
plastic bins*

Another example of shelving made from plastic bins.

Tilted shelf with labelled cans.

POLES AND BAGS

Poles can be useful for things other than plants and lights. Try a suspension pole in a corner to solve the stuffed-animal problem. Hang the pets from small pegboard hooks which fit into the holes you have drilled up and down the pole. (Use screw-in cup hooks and you won't even need a drill.) Tie a ribbon around the neck of each toy. The pole could also be hung from a hook in the ceiling.

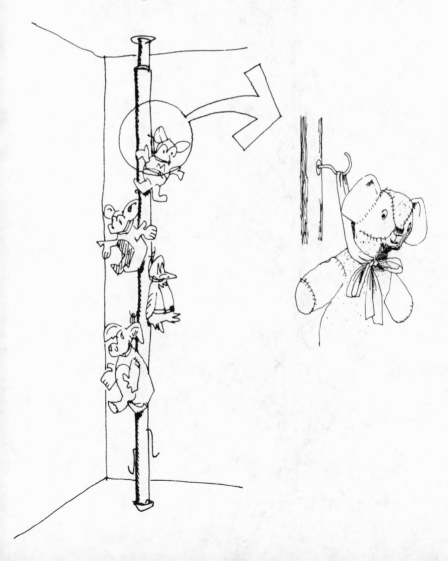

Our county library used the coat racks to hang bags of toys and games. The rack was made with a large, 2-inch diameter wooden dowel set on a stand (a Christmas-tree stand will do) and small dowels which were glued into holes drilled up and down the pole.

A 2″ x 4″ board and hooks could be used to make a similar toy pole. Toys can be easily seen through potato or grapefruit bags made from tough nylon net. Or make your own bags from a colorful print fabric. Remember, plastic bags can be dangerous.

Drawstring bags can be used in many other ways. When we're on vacation, we put all the coats in a bag to save hunting for them every time we get out of the car. Large bags are standard equipment for those who wash at a laundromat. Diane took this idea a step further by making several bags in which to separate the clothes as they were soiled and hanging them on an out-of-view wall. The bags were made from fabric similar to the wash batches: denim, terry, polyester, and flannel (for baby). She washed and dried the bags with the clothes, and used them to carry home the clean, folded clothes.

PEGBOARDS

Pegboards and hooks put utensils and tools within easy reach in work centers—office, garage, kitchen, shop, and sewing or craft areas. Pegboards can be installed behind a counter, on the end of a cupboard, on a door, or on an empty wall. I wonder, though, when I see a whole wall of cooking utensils, if they are clean enough to use for food preparation. I suggest leaving out only a few gadgets that are used every day or so. A large pegboard in the laundry area works for holding clothes hangers with clean clothes.

HANGING SHELVES AND RODS

If your house or apartment is short on enclosed shelf space, shelves made with rope and standard shelf boards may be your answer. Drill holes near the end of the shelves, slip rope through knot, and hang on two hooks. The hooks must be secured to the wood stud—even an expansion bolt won't hold a bookshelf in plasterboard (see illustration, top of page 92). A small ladder hung on chains which are anchored into the ceiling is another excellent way to create more storage space (see page 92).

A rod can be suspended with rope or chain from a higher clothes rod to add more closet space for blouses and shirts or to help small arms reach their clothes (see illustration, top of page 93).

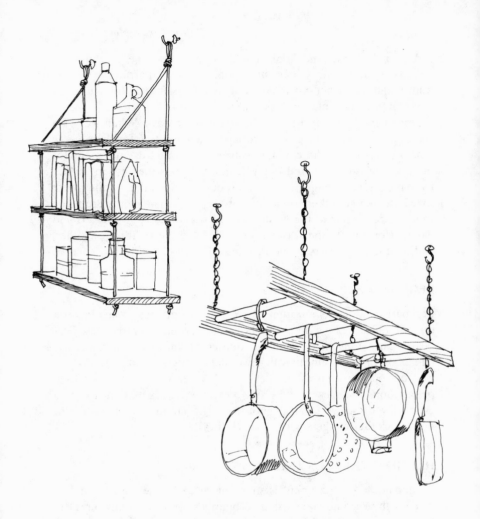

A spare rod to hang ironing or out-of-season clothes can be installed easily in an unfinished basement by nailing two strips of metal (about 1 inch wide with holes) to the ceiling joist, leaving a loop in which to slip the pipe-rod (see page 93, bottom).

If you have the right spot, install your own rods for food wraps, aluminum foil, and tear-off plastic bags, being careful to keep them near your work centers. With a hacksaw, cut a light-weight aluminum pipe and suspend it on two U-shaped brackets. Some of the wraps and bags will tear off evenly, while others may need to be cut each time with a pair of scissors (see illustration, top of page 94).

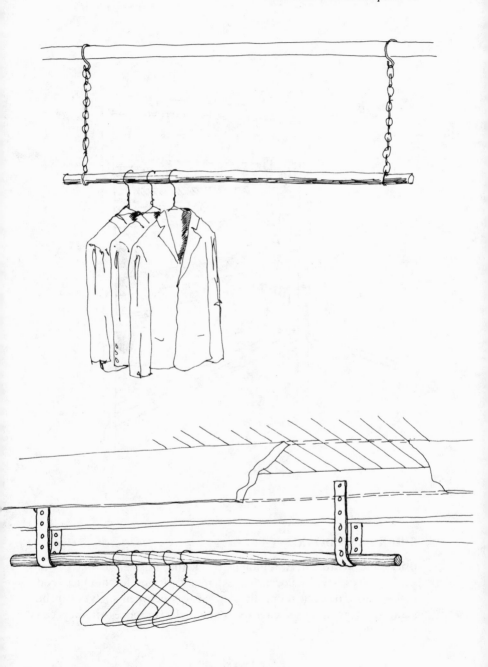

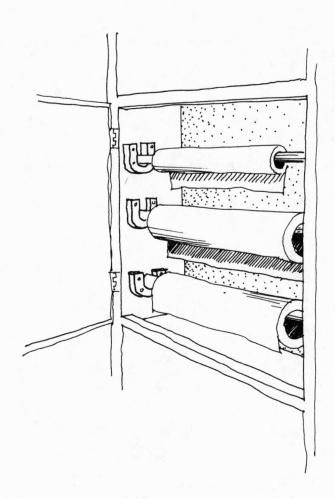

BRICKS AND BOARDS

Bricks and boards are traditional for making portable bookcases or small shelves. Cinderblocks make larger divisions for hobbies, end tables, desks, or even room dividers. Spaces between shelves can be made from anything—even logs, stone slabs, or boxes—if they can support the weight.

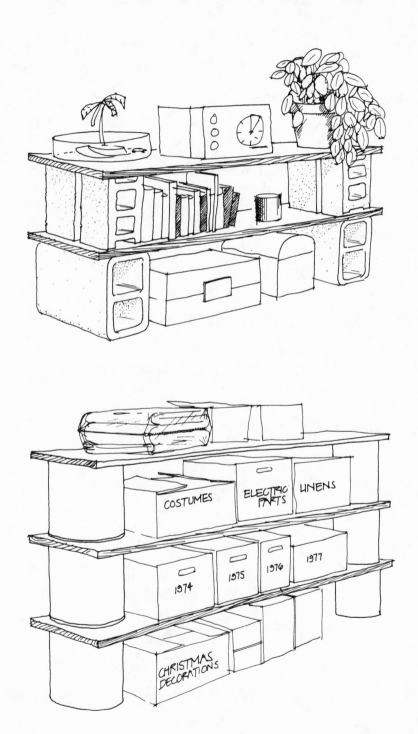

BUCKETS AND BOARDS

Buckets and boards go together to make large storage shelves. Five-gallon buckets and boards can be stacked against a wall in the basement, garage, or bedroom. Filling the buckets with something like sand or beans makes the shelves stable. One college couple had buckets-and-board shelves ceiling-high in their small living room to "ease the squeeze" and to prevent clutter. But before investing, compare the cost of sturdy metal shelving. It may be cheaper in your community than boards and buckets.

✳ FOUR ✳

Training Apprentices

*11
A Time to Work and a Time to Play

MR. WAGNER STILL LOVES HIS KIDS

As the secretary of our school stepped into the library to say hello, the former custodian, who was back for a visit, walked past. The previous week he had suffered a heart attack during school hours, and the emergency helicopter had rushed him to the hospital. The secretary said, "If Mr. Wagner had seen those spots on the window, he would have been right in here to clean them. He is one in a million: keeps everything neat, goes the extra mile, and loves the kids." Then she compared him to another custodian who also took exceptional pride in his building, but stood on guard to see that no one touched the walls, and, if they did, would throw a tantrum.

A few weeks later, when he was back to work, I had the chance to ask Mr. Wagner his secret. In his relaxed manner, he started, "Well, the kids don't usually make a mess deliberately. . . ." He had been able to separate his emotions from his work and not take it as a personal insult when the floor needed to be swept. Some messes are accidents, others are indications that a child is seeking help or attention. Even if the child did it deliberately, Mr. Wagner's attitude was the important thing. Children's messes are a result of childish irresponsibility, not deliberate disobedience. As soon as adults feel used, they rebel. A definite training program can help a child be more responsible. Children need to build skills at home just as they do in school (arithmetic before algebra and then on to trigonometry).

If Mr. Wagner were to train you or your child to take care of a school and home as he does, he would choose to have you work with him every day to see how he works and to have you try his methods.

At the same time, without knowing it, you would be learning his attitudes toward work.

Mr. Wagner's training system would be very similar to the ancient apprentice system in which children, usually in their early teens, were assigned to work under a skilled master for a period of time to learn an art or trade. After seven years, they were advanced to journeymen and then finally to masters. Often, they lived with the master and learned every attitude and appreciation of the trade.

Children are apprentices to their parents, learning valuable skills of home living. In this case, too, the master has seven years—the ages from five to twelve—or prime training time to teach the fundamental skills of personal care, simple household maintenance, and dependability. Before five years of age, children have been taught love and obedience, and their work is mostly spontaneous and voluntary. Then apprentices, with the basics under control, become journeymen. Although they are still guided by a master, they prepare for the time they will be their own masters by learning specific adult skills, finding themselves, and discovering how to get along with people. Unlike the old system, no two apprentices in the home shop go through exactly the same curriculum.

In this day and age, I prefer to call the parent a teacher or trainer rather than a master, which has such a brutal sound. If we look at ourselves as teachers and evaluate the skills each child needs, we can lovingly and systematically teach each task, at a level the child can accept, in the intimacy of a family environment. This not only helps reduce the angry emotion and frustration that accompany your child's learning period, but also gives you years of valuable help.

SET SPECIFIC GOALS

Parents who want to make good use of the apprentice system first need to write down long-range objectives. What do you expect your children to have learned when they leave your home? We often assume these objectives without stating them specifically. For example: "By the time a child leaves our home, he should know how to care for any part of the home and his own clothing, cook nutritionally, make simple household repairs, take care of the yard and garden, and so on." (Notice that I said *know how*. Don't expect a child to *do* everything—he is a trainee, not a slave.)

After you have defined the long-range goals, write them at the top of a chronological chart like the one on page 104. Now you'll need to define short-range goals and objectives in order to accomplish those lofty goals. To help you do this, think of how a school system might do it. Jefferson County Schools have a punch-out progress card that moves along with each child from grade to grade. This card indicates which detailed skills she has studied and passed. Wouldn't it be interesting to see what level our children were on at home? The chart that follows lists only a few of the skills your children should learn by the time they leave home. Use the chart as a starting point and change or expand it to fit your circumstances.

The chronological chart that follows can be used to help you assist in your child's progress toward adulthood. At the top of the chart, pencil in your long-range goals. Now, using the skills listed in the progress chart as a guide, map out which skills you would like your child to learn by a certain age. Certainly this chart should be very flexible, but it will be helpful in giving a rough idea of your child's progress and your progress as a parent/teacher. Suppose you want to teach a child to garden. When will you start? You will help the very young child investigate and understand the growing process, but when will he be given the responsibility of watering and weeding the garden or mowing the lawn? Perhaps you're thinking, "What's all the fuss about? When he is ready, I'll teach him." A child doesn't suddenly become ready on his or her sixth birthday. You need to plan and prepare him to be ready for this responsibility. Just as you plan a vacation in small steps by setting a date, making reservations, evaluating costs, and preparing clothes, education at home will reach its fullest potential only when you plan in small steps by setting goals and provide opportunities for practice at assuming responsibility in small doses, while the child is ready and willing to learn. This makes the process fun for everyone, just like going on a trip.

As in school, our children need much practice in each skill, sometimes going back to relearn. At home, we need to be flexible and reevaluate often for each child, making sure she learns every skill you've agreed is necessary. Even though there are too many varying circumstances for this to be a strict guide, you may establish a "timeline" for teaching various home responsibilities. More responsibility should be added with age and the conquest of easier skills to create a challenge, but also, more responsibility should merit more privileges.

HOME PROGRESS CARD

Personal Skills
_____dress self

_____brush teeth

_____comb hair

_____make own bed

_____keep bedroom clean

_____arrange for own haircuts, health needs, etc.

Household Skills
_____empty dishwasher

_____set table

_____clear table

_____clean bathroom

_____use broom and dustpan

_____empty wastebaskets

_____load and turn on dishwasher

_____dust without breaking

_____use a vacuum cleaner

_____wash clothes in machine

_____fold clothes neatly without wrinkles

_____polish wood

_____wash windows and walls

_____weed garden

_____water grass

_____mow lawn

_____trim trees and shrubs

_____wash car

_____iron clothes

_____do simple mending

_____proper use phone (including taking messages and making long-distance calls)

_____change vacuum belt and bag

_____replace fuse, faucet washer

Cooking Skills
_____measure properly

_____make gelatin or Jell-O

_____cook soup from can

_____make a sandwich

_____pack a cold lunch

_____make tossed salad

_____make fruit salad

_____read a recipe

_____bake a cake mix

_____bake cookies

_____bake muffins and biscuits

_____bake bread

_____mix pancakes and waffles

_____cook frozen or canned vegetables

_____prepare and cook a variety of fresh vegetables

_____fry a hamburger

_____fry a chicken

_____carve meat

_____grill or broil a steak

_____bake a roast

_____make a casserole

_____distinguish between good and spoiled foods

_____pick the freshest vegetables and fruit

_____plan and shop for balanced meals for a week

_____clean and defrost refrigerator

_____clean stove and oven

_____bottle fruit

_____freeze fruits, vegetables, and meat

_____pressure-can vegetables and meat

Money Skills
_____write a check
_____make a savings or checking-
account deposit
_____balance a checkbook
_____understand and properly use
credit card

_____compare quality and prices
when buying
_____return an item to store
properly

Navigation Skills
_____read a map
_____ride a bus or taxi
_____drive a car
_____fill tires with air

_____change a flat tire
_____check oil
_____fill radiator

Other Skills
_____knowledge of emergency first
aid
_____understanding of medicine
and the seriousness of overuse
_____swim
_____type
_____scrub, strip, and wax floors
_____shampoo carpets
_____organize a spring cleaning

_____properly hang something from
wall
_____properly use latex and enamel
paint, wood stains, and
polyurethane
_____hang wallpaper
_____clean furnace and water heater
(and light it, if gas)
_____light a stove or oven

At home, young apprentices (ages 5 to 12) learn consistency with the basic maintenance skills and personal grooming, while at school they are learning the basic concepts of reading, writing, and arithmetic. (Even though we are mostly discussing the parental role of teaching home responsibilities, it is assumed you will also give full support to children's education at school.)

One of the goals my husband and I set was to give our children the gift of reading. We did this by creating as many opportunities as possible for our children to get excited about books. We read a story to them every day, gave them books as gifts, joined a book club, went to the library every three weeks, and started reading more ourselves. It all paid off. Our two oldest daughters read a book a day and the younger ones are catching their enthusiasm.

The journeyman, having mastered the basics, is ready to start building a repertoire of pre-occupational and adult skills. For instance, this is the time you systematically teach the various cooking methods and associated cleaning procedures such as cleaning a stove top and oven. Don't forget meal planning and food selection. Several times we have ended up with cabbage salad instead of lettuce salad when the children shopped. To prevent food poisoning, your child will need to know how to tell when meat or vegetables are spoiled. The child needs experience with simple repairs: replacing the vacuum belt, changing a faucet washer, even oiling a squeaky door. Your training

---

CHRONOLOGICAL CHART FOR
SETTING LONG- AND SHORT-RANGE GOALS

(Pencil in the age at which you think your child should begin learning each skill. A few suggestions are shown, but only as examples, because each child is different.)

	Age	Goal
Journeyman: learns pre-occupational and adult skills, becomes more independent, and matures socially.	18	
	17	
	16	begin driving car
	15	
	14	start car repairs and maintenance
	13	
	12	begin mowing lawn
	11	
Apprentice: learns fundamental skills of personal care, simple household chores, and dependability.	10	learn to operate washing machine
	9	
	8	begin cooking and assisting in kitchen
	7	
	6	
	5	begin daily family chores
Time of love and obedience, when work is spontaneous and mostly voluntary.	4	start making bed alone
	3	start to dress self, encourage
	2	independence
	1	

program should include opportunities to use and misuse money through allowances and paid jobs. Helping a child plan and shop for clothes is good experience in comparing prices and quality. If your child has $35 to build up her wardrobe, how can she get the most for her money? Creating circumstances where the child can buy or make gifts is also a growing experience in understanding the value of things.

As you assess your child's needs and aptitudes, make enjoyable and pre-occupational opportunities available, such as music, typing, woodworking, arts and crafts, sewing, or mechanics, which will be helpful at home or at work. No journeyman will learn every technique and skill necessary for adulthood, but if he has learned enough to have confidence in his ability to learn more, and if he has learned the essentials to survive, he will continue his learning progression as an adult. Although you, as parent, should guide your child through all this planning, the journeyman, your child, has a great deal to say about these decisions and goals.

It's never too late to start a home training program—just assess your child's needs, set your goals according to the child's age, readiness, emotional and physical level, and start. You are going to be doing many things during these eighteen years, so why not have a direction in mind. Children gain confidence when they see the effect of their efforts and realize that they can complete a task. The parent is rewarded by seeing the children's growth in independence and by receiving help with the home work load.

When they are training apprentices, parents need to remember Mr. Wagner and show patience and love. Children are not perfect. Parents need not be "used" by sloppy, ungrateful children, but remember, learning the basics for survival takes many years. The home is supposed to be a child's refuge from the world, not just a sweat shop.

Even though your child is expected to finish assigned chores (see Chapter 12, Teaching Job Skills), call her back to finish a job or pick up a coat only after a specific infringement. Follow-up is important, but you can't constantly be riding her, or you're taking over her responsibility and you will become an unpleasant image associated with scoldings and force. Give a child time for rest and recreation (R & R). This may mean keeping a list of unfinished assignments for her to do during her next work time so she can have time off from training pressures.

Teach your child the concept that a certain amount of cleaning and maintenance will need to be done to take care of things no one is directly accountable for. We don't say, "Who ate on this dish? Come and wash it." Treat the job of washing dinner dishes as a unit. If I tell my nine-year-old son to clean the family room, he'll try, "But I didn't get all those books out!" "I know, son, just pick them up." Sometimes, though, a parent must be responsible for a younger child's messes to keep resentment from smoldering in older children until the younger one is responsible enough to care for himself.

Mr. Wagner, the school custodian, still loves his kids when they make a mess; you can too.

Practical Application:

Prepare a "time line" with a long-range goal showing what you hope your child will have completed when he or she leaves your home and showing approximately the age he or she will begin learning each task. Review it at least twice a year.

*12
Teaching Job Skills

As a parent, you know it is faster to do a job yourself than to see that a child does it. "Why do you insist that your children make their beds?" a man once challenged. "What does it matter? If it bothers you so much, why not do it yourself or just close their door? Why do parents fuss so much about beds?" It's not really the beds we are concerned about, but it's one of our efforts to help the child mature into a *responsible adult*. It isn't difficult to learn to make a bed. The accomplishment is in making it *every* day. If children have control over little things, they will be ready to learn control over big things. Self-discipline can be taught in small steps. What an advantage it is when one learns to do something one doesn't necessarily want to do. My theory is that children who make their beds every day will go to work every day as adults.

As a parent, I find several reasons for having children make their beds every day. Children need the training that comes through learning to work and having responsibility. Mastering the basic home skills gives them motivation for new learning endeavors. It can be better than receiving a huge endowment of money at age twenty-one. Besides the wonderful advantages for the child of teaching self-discipline and learning the basic skills, there are benefits for the parents. Adults can't be efficient or hard-working enough to keep up the house and do meaningful things with their children if the children are unwilling and inconsiderate. Parents need help, and if the training is successful, the children's efforts will be measurable. One more reason for making the bed is that it looks better—which can improve a child's self-image.

Because of our modern culture, both boys and girls need to learn all the home tasks. They may run into trouble if they are indoctrinated into believing that dishes are woman's work and yard care is man's work. We can't guarantee that a boy won't have to iron or that a girl will always have someone around to fill the radiator or change the oil. A woman who can't balance a bank statement and a man who can't cook a meal are unnecessarily dependent. Therefore, it is assumed in these discussions that boys and girls will learn almost all the same skills.

FINGER PLAYS FOR CHORES

How many reminders did you give this morning to your children? "Is your bed made?" "Have you brushed your teeth?" "Go comb your hair!" Why should the parent have this responsibility? Teach young children to take on their own responsibilities with a simple reminder system on their fingers.

How does it work? The parent teaches the child a sequence of key words or phrases, one for each finger. Each day, the child runs through the list on his fingers and does each task. When he is finished, he is ready to go to school or play.

To begin this in your home, list the tasks that need to be done every day. Pick a noun to be the key word to represent each job. Arrange

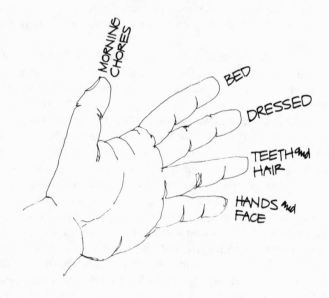

them in order of sequence. Brushing teeth and washing could come before dressing, to prevent splashes on clean clothes. The sequence we have used in our family is: (1) hands and face, (2) teeth and hair, (3) dressed (including shoes and socks), (4) bed (including room pickup), (5) morning chore or just toys for the younger children. We didn't include eating breakfast because we don't have a problem in that area. Use the same set of words for all children in a family. Added responsibility can be attached to the symbol word as the child matures, but don't try to change the key words. For instance, under the third category, bed, a four-year-old isn't asked to vacuum his bedroom, but by the time he is seven, vacuuming might be part of his responsibility.

When the child needs a reminder, the parent says, "What have you finished so far?" After going over the sequence of words on her fingers, the child will answer, "Well, I've swept the stairs and made my bed, but I still have to brush my teeth." She has been the one to recognize what must be done, and she is on the way to self-rule.

This memory device of learning the morning routine on fingers can be started even on seven-year-olds, and will last a lifetime. The most important point is that the child learns to answer the questions, "Am I finished yet?" and "What must I still do?"

We started teaching our youngest child personal responsibility at two and a half years. After dressing him, I look his little hand in mine and pointed to one finger at a time, "Now, Mattie, let's see what you have to do" (like playing piggy-wiggy). "Hands and face?" (He nods yes whether he had done it or not). "Teeth and hair?" "No, let's do that now." When he finished brushing, we began again. "Dressed?" "Yes, and your shoes are on too! Good boy! Bed?" (Nods yes.) "No, I'll help you. Toys? We'll pick up your books after we make the bed." Taking him by the hand, I'd lead him lovingly through each activity. Naturally he was too young to make his bed, but he stood next to me while I did it. In a year or so, he would be better able to climb up to the head of the bed and pull up the covers. When we were all finished, I'd give him lots of praise and then tell him he could play because all his chores were finished. He left feeling grown up and successful.

After the basic hygiene and chores are taken care of, a child is free from parental promptings. He feels rewarded for his accomplishment because he is ready for whatever opportunity comes up. He can go for a ride to the store or play with a friend. Once the basic responsibilities are established, parents can feel like more than just reminders—they can be leaders instead of herders.

CHORE CHARTS

Setting up a long-range goal and dividing it into yearly and monthly goals will help organize children's chores. Children prefer knowing ahead of time exactly what they must do and want to keep that chore for a week or two. They recognize that if you do something often, it gets easier. There are several methods for assigning and rotating jobs.

Before assigning chores, I looked around for areas of the home that needed daily care, that children could master, and that required less than ten minutes (their time). As it came out, the morning chores were the minimum maintenance for the main living areas of the home. The evening chores centered around dinner preparation, because everyone already helps with cleanup after dinner.

Rotating or pocket-type charts are good reminders. Our Chore Chart has two rows of pockets; the first one for morning and the second for evening. Each Monday the chores are rotated. When the young child who doesn't yet have a regular assignment has a willing heart, find something she can do without getting hurt, such as washing the plastic dishes or shaking a rug. By the time she starts school, she will be taking turns in the regular daily responsibilities.

There are hundreds of possibilities for the Chore Charts to fit varying family circumstances. Try giving an only child a morning and evening job as shown on the circular chart, rotating the jobs so he gets some variety, but don't expect an only child to do all eight chores every day. To adapt the chart to fit the quantity of work and number of workers, simply change the number of pockets or pie-shape divisions on the chart.

As you are looking for chores to assign, consider whether the task is within the child's abilities. Remember, children can often make bigger messes than they can clean up by themselves. They need assistance and encouragement to conquer the chore or clean up the mess. Assign the chore so the child can take care of it independently without waiting for someone else to do another part of it first. Every child needs to succeed. Follow the steps of training as discussed later; even a six-year-old can clean up a bathroom very well.

You can be flexible and still consistent. Your child will balk, cry, throw tantrums, and try to escape if he thinks there is a chance he won't have to do something today, especially as you begin assigning chores. *The secret is to be consistent in requiring some help from each child every day.* Having a regular time every day for this work helps establish consistency in getting it done. Some days their help will be needed more than others. Holidays, Sundays, and birthdays might be exceptions—after all, you like time off, too. Decide what you expect and then stick to it, but at the same time be flexible and understanding. Some parents get hung up here because they aren't consistent in performing their own responsibilities. As your child matures, you will need to adjust the chores, change your requirements, and include her in your decision making.

In the beginning, it will take more time to teach your children to work than if you simply did it yourself; but in the end, you will have more time to do things *with* them.

STEP BY STEP

Do you expect your children to learn the basic skills of home living only by example? They will need to be trained. After you have decided which chore to teach, start the training gently. Make the learning time pleasant. Use lots of specific praise and positive reinforcement. "Mattie, you did a good job polishing the mirror." Anger, force, and physical or verbal abuse will instill the wrong attitudes about work.

Explaining the job and writing it down will save misunderstandings about what is a completed task. The secret is to divide the work into small portions and then show and explain each part carefully. Posting the job specifications on a chart in the closet as on page 52 will develop self-evaluation. As the child matures, the job can be expanded. For example, a five-year-old cleaning the bathroom might scour the sink, polish the chrome, and shake the rug. A ten-year-old could handle the additional chores of mopping the floor, washing the towels, and polishing the mirrors.

In the beginning, complete the job together, praising the child's efforts. Gradually withdraw your help until he can succeed alone. Teach him to see what needs to be done: "Now stand back here at the

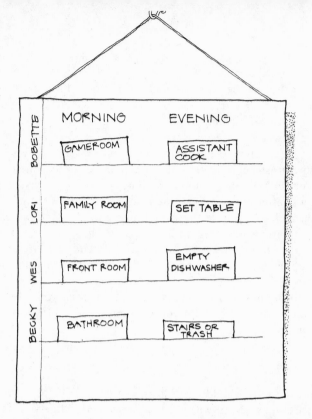

Children's Work Assignment Charts (here and on opposite page). These jobs were chosen from daily Minimum Maintenance (MM) for the main living areas of the home and require about 10 minutes. They are in addition to the responsibilities of their own bedrooms. Chores are rotated every Monday morning. Each child is responsible for thoroughly cleaning his or her bedroom on the weekend.

door, son, and see how much better it looks. What else needs to be done? What do you think about the open drawer?" Get him to tell you. Performing a task is easy if he knows how.

Training won't be very successful if the supervisor is involved with his or her own work while the children are supposed to be doing their chores. Be available to supervise—not like a taskmaster with a whip, but to direct, help, praise, and motivate. See that each child is victorious; it is great motivation. Restrain yourself and *never redo a job* you have passed. If a child is having a difficult time, ask "What would you like me to do to help you?" This way you neither assume her responsibility nor abandon her.

Use the basic principles of minimum maintenance. Teach children that they should start with the biggest item and work down to the smaller articles; closed doors and drawers look neater; things must be picked up before getting out more; they must not start more than they can clean up; and it's easier to put things away while they are in hand.

Guide your child into good work habits by setting time limits. Chores must be completed before 8 A.M. on school days and 10 A.M. on Saturday, is one family's rule. Another one says grooming and chores must be finished before TV, school, or other projects. First things first! Children can't work forever; they want to see the end. When they are finished, turn them loose. Adding more assignments will squelch their incentive and punish efficiency. Don't spring a cleaning day on the kids; give them advance notice. "Mom, let me know my assignment so I can work it in," said one teen. Children are more likely to get work done if there is a regular time to do it every day.

Inspecting the job gives opportunity for verbal rewards and makes children feel that their assignments are important. After an acceptable

Rotating Work Chart

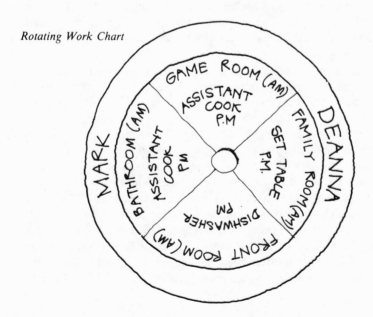

level of competence has been reached, withdrawing the inspection and accepting a verbal expression of completion will build integrity. If a job should fail the inspection, criticize the job, not the child. Gently guide the child in the areas that need additional effort.

During the school year, when children are concentrating on schoolwork, emphasize keeping up with the regular little daily chores. School vacations might be used to teach new skills like washing walls or baking cookies. In June, set goals and make plans as to what new skills you intend to integrate with the fun during the summer. This could include summer classes in art, mechanics, and the like.

Teaching the job is easy, but guiding the child to efficiency takes great patience and diplomacy. One frustrated parent asked, "What do I do with Joe—he drags out his morning chores until two in the afternoon?" There are two points to consider here. First, does Joe need more parental help to succeed? We assume that because he knows *how* to do a chore, he can get it done. It takes years for a child to learn to *follow through,* which is an important element of good work habits. Joe may need assistance time after time, but each success helps develop the habit of following through with a task. If he needs help, remember to ask him what he needs you to do. Second, to solve Joe's problem, stop and evaluate whether he is having trouble getting his work done because he has too heavy a work load. Can he see the end of the work? Cutting back on the work and rebuilding his self-esteem may be necessary.

Most children possess natural enthusiasm for self-competition and find satisfaction in their accomplishments. Capitalize on this by pointing out these good feelings. "Let's see if we can beat the clock and have this room straight in fifteen minutes." Then when it's finished, "We did it! Doesn't it feel good?" Clear, firm, friendly insistence on proper performance can help teach diligent effort in all the child does.

With all the seriousness of work, keep your sense of humor. Never be so uptight about things that you can't joke about them. Remember, "In every task that must be done, there's an element of fun." Look for the fun, or make your own. Make it as easy as possible for the child: teach her how, help her succeed, and inspect when necessary. Tell her when she does a good job. Create an incentive (it becomes a bribe when you say *if*). Children need outside motivation until they are mature enough to generate incentives from within. Divide tasks into small enough parts so that they can master them. Success is a reward in and of itself.

Practical Application:

Design a program with at least one home responsibility in addition to care of the child's own bedroom. Make a visual schedule, probably a chart, showing:

1. what the job is for now
2. how long it will last (1 to 2 weeks)
3. what the next week's responsibility will be
4. what time of day this job will be started or completed

Follow up with help and inspections until the child has completed the task at least three times successfully.

*13
Cures for the Bedroom

Johnny's room is a disaster: clothes, toys, and books are scattered all over, drawers are open, and the bed is unmade. What are parents to do? If they constantly nag Johnny about cleaning his bedroom, he resents it and the communication gap grows. If they shut the door and wait for Johnny to get ready to clean, he may learn to accept a sloppy way of life. His self-image slumps: "I am a messy person." The parents who pick up and clean after a careless child have the satisfaction of a clean house but are bypassing the child's lessons in personal responsibility. Johnny will grow up expecting tidiness but will see it as the responsibility of others, not realizing any part of it as his responsibility. My theory is that it is better to *help* a child with his room, so he may learn to like order and feel good about himself, than to withdraw, close the door, and allow him to live without any order.

What causes these bedroom problems? You may increase your understanding by stopping to evaluate the causes. Does your child have all his belongings in his room? It's usually easier for parents to keep their room in order because they have other places for treasures and equipment. The parents' domain is the whole house; the child's domain is just his room. Perhaps there's *too much* for the room? Is there another spot for some of it, perhaps in other areas? When it has been out of his sight for a while, he may realize he really doesn't need it and it could be disposed of at a garage sale or given to Santa's Workshop.

Consider the physical structure of your child's bedroom. Is there enough space available? Perhaps storage space could be added by installing low shelves, shelves at the end of the closet, knickknack shelves, a bulletin board, chests, low hooks and rods, or cinderblock and board units for books and hobbies. A child needs help creating a place for everything. Keep games and toys separated in small boxes or bags. With him, organize his collections into shoe boxes in the closet or create displays for his walls.

Make it as easy as possible for the child to keep her room clean. Use bedspreads with long, horizontal cording that marks the edges of the bed. Quilts are popular and decorative and can double as a spread and blanket, making bedmaking a breeze. Pull the bed away from the wall so the child can get around it, or tuck in the covers on the wall side. Be sure there is a wastebasket and a large clothes hamper in the room. Dividers can be used in the drawers to separate socks, underwear, belts, and pajamas.

Collections and hobbies must be held to a minimum. I know all about exposing children to many talents and making them well rounded, but if you start a new collection or hobby every birthday and Christmas, you are asking for a bedroom problem. Encourage children by adding some new stamps, coins, or tools to their existing collections.

Make a child's room attractive so he can take pride in it. From time to time, add something special, such as a picture, or new wallpaper or paint. Even cement walls can be painted. Involve the child in these redecorating plans. Don't forget to make this time together fun—talk about pleasant things or even sing so the child enjoys your time together.

Every child needs bounds and limits. School papers can be contained in a soup-can box. When it is full, the child must go through it, keeping a few special ones and throwing away the rest. A bulletin board holds just so many finger paintings; the older ones must be thrown out to make room for the new ones. Only so many models can go on a shelf; the others must be stored. Set limits on how many clothes he will have. What little boy needs fifteen pairs of jeans, even if they *were* good hand-me-downs. He will have trouble keeping his drawers straight if they are too full, and clean clothes will tend to be tossed into the hamper. To save room in the closet, hang matching pants or skirts and tops together. Our son has even asked that I hang his jeans with matching shirts, and he does look better these days. Put out-of-season clothes away. In DeAnna's home, each child has two fruit boxes in the top of his or her closet: one marked Out of Season and the other marked Grow Into. DeAnna cycles out the outgrown clothing as it passes through the laundry and either puts it in the younger child's Grow Into box or puts it into the charity basket. If the child doesn't wear something, remove it; it is taking up unnecessary space.

One frustrated parent took everything out of a daughter's bedroom except the bed and eight days' worth of clothing until she could keep that much straight.

Help children keep a few mementoes, treasures, and special items. They need guidance to know what pictures and programs will still be treasures in ten years. It is nice to have a few things to show the next generation. Create a special place for these treasures. We prefer not to keep these "scrap-book" boxes in the childrens' bedroom, where visiting playmates or younger children might damage them.

Be careful about throwing away your children's belongings without asking or having their help with the decision after they are four or five years old. How would you feel? One of my Cub Scouts was showing his pinewood derby car to his sixteen-year-old friend. "Boy, I remember when I made my car. Wait a minute and I'll get it." A very sad teen came back fifteen minutes later. "Mom threw it away."

Marsha said she had solved the "bedroom dilemma" by cleaning out her son's bedroom while he is at school. The problem is that if her son never learns the delicate art of what to keep and what to get rid of, he may grow up to be one of those adults who just can't get rid of anything.

A room that is messy for several days signals a need for parental help in cleaning and organizing. Children are capable of making a bigger mess than they can clean up. Help them divide it into small areas. "First let's pick up the blocks and then the crayons." Patiently help them see what needs to be done, help them conquer, and eventually they can take over complete care of their own room.

Practical Application:
Look and discover what is causing the mess and propose a solution.

Toys:
_____Are there too many stuffed animals?
_____Are the little parts and pieces spread out in various places?
_____Do the big things have a place?

Bed:
_____Is it hard to make?
_____Is it too close to the wall?
_____Does he or she need more training in the bed-making skill?

Clothes:
_____Are the drawers too full?
_____Is there a hamper? Is it large enough?
_____Are last years', this years' and next years' clothes mixed together?
_____Does he or she need more drawer space now that he or she is older?
_____Could any of these clothes be hung in the closet?
_____Is the closet too full?
_____Is the rod too high or too low?
_____Is there space in the closet for another rod, a small chest, or shelves?
_____Is there a place for the shoes?

Books and school papers:
_____Do they all belong in this room?
_____Are shelves needed?
_____Is there a place for homework?
_____What about a place for graded papers?
_____Is it too full?
_____Is there need for a bulletin board or display area?
_____Is there a surface for doing homework and creative crafts?

Get together with the child, decide what to do with the toys, clothes, and books, and let her or him help you organize them.

*14
Carrots and Sticks

The prime motivator for success in changing children's behavior is showing and expressing appreciation. Children change their behavior to receive rewards or strokes. Strokes can be positive or negative, and children prefer one over the other by the time they are seven or eight, depending on which satisfied their need for attention. Negative responses don't bring about positive behavior, they only reinforce the undesirable. Strokes can be general: "You are a super individual." Strokes can be specific: "You did a nice job washing the car." Strokes come in varying degrees of vigor: "I'm proud of you" or *"I'm really proud of you!"* More emphasis or emotion means the reward is greater. Positive strokes are the best rewards. We all seek them, we can save them up, and they are the building blocks of self-confidence.

General strokes are difficult to accept. "I hear you are the best den mother in Denver," is a hard compliment to respond to. If the leader knows she can't compare to those ideals, she can't honestly accept the compliment and may begin listing all the reasons she is not the best den leader. If she had been told, "My son had so much fun last week in Cub Scouts—he really likes you," the woman could have accepted that specific stroke. A general stroke—"You are a good boy"—is so unmeasurable that the child may feel obligated to prove you wrong. Or it may mean, to him, that he can be a good boy only when he does exactly what the parent desires, thereby taking away his individuality.

By making your positive strokes deal with specific details, the child knows what she or he did right. "I can tell you worked especially hard making your bed this morning," or "I was so pleased to see you put your plate in the dishwasher without being asked." A stroke complimenting a physical trait or something a child really isn't responsible for, such as, "Becky, your hair is such a lovely color of red," isn't nearly as meaningful as a compliment directed toward her ability or personality: "Becky, you take such good care of your hair," or "It's fun to be with you." Positive reinforcement, strokes, compliments, and praise will do a great deal in helping your child learn to do household chores or take care of personal grooming.

Until your child has established good habits and is self-motivated, you will need to use many varieties of rewardable activities (keep changing the carrot). Put something less desirable before something more desirable. "When you have your pajamas on, we will read a story." "After you have finished your bedroom, we will go to the library." Remember: the word *if* signals bribery or threat.

No matter how exciting, how easy, fun, fair, and organized you have made the work, you must anticipate that the rule will be tested. Parent, be ready by deciding how it will be enforced. The outside world is filled with consequences. If you don't pay the phone bill, your service will be disconnected. When you walk on thin ice, you will fall through. Whether you are an adult or a child, if you stick a nail in an electric outlet, you will get shocked. These are natural consequences. Using natural laws as discipline whenever possible is most effective. When there isn't a natural consequence or if it is too dangerous, logical consequences can be structured by the parent. Examples: "If you misuse the car, you must turn in your keys." "When you cause a spill, whether on purpose or by accident, you must clean it up." Learning to use consequences is like learning to use a new appliance. It takes effort; so think ahead. This type of discipline keeps you on the level of teacher rather than executioner. Taking time to determine the consequence may mean leaving the scene until you can logically think it through.

Our eight-year-old repeatedly left his dresser drawers open. It made the room look messy and it was dangerous for his younger brother, who slept next to the dresser. Rather than restrict TV privileges or issue a paddling, which had nothing to do with his neglectful habit, I calmly said, "Wes, you seem to be having such a hard time keeping these drawers closed, I guess you need a training session. I want you to practice opening and closing these drawers ten times. Watch me first." It was so ridiculous that we were both laughing before he was finished. He got my point and it worked better than angrily dumping the contents on the floor.

Requiring a repayment for unnecessary service from a parent may greatly reduce the work. If a child doesn't finish a chore and it can't be left until he gets home, he must do a makeup chore, such as sweeping the porch. This works especially well for redeeming an only coat or shoe which the parent had to pick up. When clean clothes are thrown into the laundry rather than being hung up, have the child wash those clothes by hand. To make certain the child knows what brought about the consequence, include a time to talk. Asking him to restate the broken rule is one of the most effective tricks. It removes misunderstandings and reinforces his memory for next time.

Issuing allowances will teach children wise buying habits, encourage responsibility, and promote generosity, but money doesn't make a good disciplinary rod. Each child might receive 25¢ per year of age each month (a ten-year-old would get $2.50). After the age of twelve, they are usually earning supplemental income. The allowance may come with restrictions regarding sweet treats and gum, but it should not be connected with the completion of chores or good behavior. We expect each child to take part in the maintenance and upkeep of the inside and outside of our home as part of the responsibility of being a member of the family. Therefore, we pay them only for jobs that we would normally pay someone else to come in and do.

By including your children in the family decision-making process, you will help prepare them for making their own decisions when they grow up. As your children mature, adjust the rules, change the requirements, and increase your flexibility. It might be better for a teen to have the larger weekend chore of cleaning the refrigerator than daily vacuuming of the living room.

Again, every child tests the rules, so plan ahead. Serve generous amounts of appreciation and strokes to your apprentices. It will build their self-esteem and help them know you love them even when they aren't perfect.

MORE INCENTIVES

Do you realize what five little M & M candies can do? They can motivate a child to sleep in his own bed, overcome the fear of going to Sunday-school class alone, or get him to flush the toilet and wash his hands. They act as incentives and immediate rewards. Creating proper incentives is challenging, but it results in positive changes when it is coupled with strokes. We have heard of the amazing successes made with slow and retarded children by issuing immediate rewards. Special-learning classes offer small prizes which the students earn for good work. Immediate rewards can also be a tool to improve behavior in normal children. I took great interest in a book by N.H. Azrin, Ph.D., and R.M. Foxx, Ph.D. called *Toilet Training in Less than a Day* (Simon & Schuster, 1974). The author suggests spending the day alone with the child, having him train a doll, and carefully rewarding each of the child's acceptable actions with candy or drink until he can go through the whole routine by himself. Although I was not successful in toilet training our son in one day, we made remarkable progress and I learned a great deal about incentives.

Important principles for using the incentive plan are: (1) work with only one behavior change at a time, (2) keep the task simple, (3) make the reward minimal, (4) be unwaveringly consistent in giving the reward only when *all* the desired behavior is performed.

How do the M & M candies work? "I have five M & M's here in my pocket for you after Sunday school if you stay in your class." If he doesn't quite make it, say, "I'm sorry, son, perhaps next week you can stay with your teacher." Don't give the reward unless he completes the behavior. You may need a gentle one-time reminder of the pending reward beforehand: "I hope you sleep in your bed all night so you can have five chocolate-coated raisins in the morning." (Repeating the incentive over and over turns it into a bribe.) In the morning, praise and approval come with the reward: "I'm so proud of you for sleeping in your bed. I knew you could do it. Doesn't it make you feel good?" Incentives don't have to keep getting bigger, like bribes. It took a total of only twenty-five M & M candies for our son to go to class alone. Soon he forgot all about the candy reward and found enough reward from our attention discussing what he had learned.

Any special privilege can become an incentive, but for children, immediate incentives work better than long-range rewards. The leverage will be lost if you are doling out handfuls of candy every time you turn around. Just work on one behavior change at a time, and the reward need not be edible. At Glennon Height Elementary School, the class with the cleanest room hosts a "mop doll" for a week. Venturing into new territory can be scary, so a reward is used to help the child try harder and succeed. Negative threats or comments only reinforce the undesirable behavior. Keep it positive, be each other's cheerleaders.

Pam used the incentive method to motivate a habit change: taking

off clothes right side out (saves lots of time on laundry day!). Instead of nagging, she packed a suitcase with Dad's big pajama bottoms, socks, and sweat shirt. At family council, the game was to put on Dad's clothes and take them off *right side out.* Each child who was successful (and she made sure they all were) received a coupon redeemable for a treat. Then Pam explained that another coupon could be earned for each person whose clothes came through the laundry on wash day all right side out. After issuing success coupons for only four weeks, Pam had modified an undressing habit that had amounted to many work hours for her.

Sometimes, if you are watching, motivation opportunities just accidentally happen. One mother whose teenage son had extreme difficulty keeping his room clean found a clue in her son's request for a good feather pillow. "Yes, son, you can have this pillow as long as you make your bed every day." On other occasions, the parents had tried offering him the moon without any improvement in the bedroom. Part of this incentive game is finding the right key. One day the boy forgot to make the bed and, without comment, the pillow was taken back. That day the boy made the bed when he got home from school, redeeming the pillow, and it didn't happen again. By this time, the boy had learned he could make the bed quickly, and he liked it better that way—the incentive had helped him over the hang-up. When he saw the bed was neatly made, he felt good, he knew it pleased his parents, and his self-esteem shot up.

Children want to succeed, but sometimes they need to know that their parents will help them with reminders, encouragement, and love. Being parents is not an easy game, and you're never sure if you have won.

Little Sarah's parents offered her anything she wanted at the store if she would give up sucking her thumb. Because she was old enough and ready to exercise that self-discipline, she overcame the habit and earned her reward, a new doll. Her solution was to put her thumb right by her cheek when she slept, but never in her mouth.

A spoiled three-year-old boy once brought his father charging out of the chair when he called his mother "pig." As with most three-year-olds, this little fellow was experimenting with words, and the word "pig" got quite a reaction. The father associated an entirely different meaning with the word than the boy, who was thinking of Miss Piggy, one of the muppets on TV. The boy was severely reprimanded, but because of the attention he received (even though it was negative), he used the word more often. He tried it in front of his grandparents and at the grocery store—you know what they thought! It took great self-control for his parents to ignore the boy and give no "reward" when the word was used. It took three or four months after the initial episode for the word finally to slip from his regular vocabulary.

THIS CERTIFIES THAT YOU MAY REDEEM THIS COUPON FOR A SPECIAL TREAT BECAUSE ALL YOUR CLOTHES WERE TURNED RIGHT SIDE OUT THIS WEEK

Practical Application:

Pick out a problem area—something you feel is necessary and desirable for the child to do, such as keeping his room clean. Replace all the past negative attitudes and experiences by offering the child something the child desires when he has completed the dreaded task. Make the reward desirable, but still allow him to make the choice. (You can't make a child do anything.) "At one o'clock, everyone in the family whose room is cleaned and vacuumed can go with us for a family swim." When the time arrives, only those who have completed the task get the reward, even if it means hiring a baby-sitter. Be firm.

Measure the success of this behavior modification by checking at the end of four weeks and eight weeks to count how many times the child has chosen to complete the task and has received the reward. If she has chosen to perform the task and receive the reward more often than not, your behavior modification is working.

FIVE

Taste, Nutrition, and Money

*15
Good Food

If you had only $25, how long could you eat? Would you go out to a fancy restaurant, or would you carefully plan a food budget? Many meals could be planned for $25, but would these meals be nutritionally sound? One mother actually fed her family nothing but popcorn and Kool-Aid for two weeks, while another served only pumpkin. Did these meals provide the energy for active play, growing bodies, and alert minds? Pumpkin is a better food than popcorn, but if it had been served with cabbage (for vitamin C) and bread or oatmeal or even pinto beans, everyone would have been better fed. Cost alone is not an indication of good food, but low-cost foods chosen for nutritive value will pay larger dividends in health than expensive foods chosen at random. Saving money is important, but first we need to talk about nutrition.

GUIDELINES FOR DIET

The U.S. Department of Agriculture's new guidelines for the American diet state: "Cut down on sugar, salt, fat, and meat. Increase vegetables, fruits, grains, and cereals."

Sugar and salt are the most widely used food additives, and we hardly consider them dangerous. The problem with salt is that it contains sodium, which contributes to high blood pressure—the painless killer with no symptoms until it's too late. Salt looks so harmless and it is everywhere—on the table, in your soup, and in nearly every packaged food you buy. By eating less salt, you can again know the real taste of food. Using only salt limits you to one flavor. There are other spices and herbs available: garlic and onion, oregano, curry, cumin, and basil. With a little experimentation and practice, you might not even miss the salt.

The average American consumes 137 pounds of sugar a year—nearly a sixth of her or his total food intake. If you buy sugar by the bag or box, you may ask yourself, "If I am not buying 137 pounds of sugar, where am I getting it?" The answer is that you're getting it from sweet drinks, candy, gelatin, cookies, crackers, rolls, dry cereals, lunch meats, hot dogs, and catsup. Soft drinks are the leading source of sugar consumption among teenage boys—almost 50 pounds a year per teenager. Try reducing the amount of sugar in your recipes, or switch to honey and use half as much. Fill in gaps by eating more fresh vegetables and fruit. Try eating fruit for dessert, as many Europeans do. True, an orange may cost more than a Twinkie, but consider the savings over the long term: fewer trips to the dentist and doctor, less medicine, and more vitality. Many people eat raisins in their cereal instead of adding sugar and pour puréed fruit over waffles and pancakes instead of using syrup.

Fat has many names: grease, lard, oil, shortening, and bacon drippings. Frequently you can't even see it. Fat is hidden in whole milk. It is the marbling in steak and the white specks in hamburger. Butter and margarine are mainly fat, and oil is entirely fat. Fats in the diet come from two sources—(1) fats occurring naturally in foods such as in whole milk, cheese, nuts, seeds, meat, poultry, fish, chocolate, etc; and (2) fats and oils added in preparing foods such as fried foods, pastries, gravies, salad dressings, etc. All fats, no matter what the source, have the same caloric value—double the number of calories, ounce-for-ounce, as other foods. Though a small amount of fat is necessary, Americans have been fooled into thinking that unsaturated fats don't count. We can tell this from the statistics that show that the consumption of unsaturated fat products is up in the same degree that the use of natural saturated fats is down. Yes, the polyunsaturated fats are *better* for your heart and circulatory systems, but they still contain the same number of calories. It has been recommended that we reduce the total intake of fats to give a better nutritional balance among protein, fats and carbohydrates in our diet.

How can we help reduce the fat in your diet? Switch to low-fat milk, cheese, and yogurt; eat more fish, chicken (without the skin), turkey, beans, and other legumes. When you eat meat, keep it lean and cut off the extra fat. Remember that when animal fat cools inside your system and arteries, it turns solid again. Use only a few drops of oil in the frying pan or spray it with a non-stick coating. Put in less oil than a recipe calls for. Limit nuts, peanuts, and peanut butter, which contain considerable amounts of fat. Try yogurt in place of sour cream, butter, and mayonnaise (it's easy to make your own yogurt). You can show your family you love them in many ways other than serving rich foods.

Once it could be said that bread is the staff of life, but in this country, we have gotten away from the use of bread and other grain products, partly becaue they require so much preparation time. Whole grain foods are good sources of protein and also fiber helps prevent constipation and some chronic diseases of the large intestine. We can increase our use as recommended by our government's dietitians, by adding them to breakfast and lunch menus for the active parts of our day. Even though it's more effort, cooked cereals, muffins, toast, pancakes, and waffles can be rotated with your regular breakfast menu. Then you can have a sandwich for lunch and pasta or taco shells with dinner and you have met your daily requirements. Now if you add those grains, you'll need to eliminate some other foods, preferably sugar, and part of your meat, or you'll gain extra weight. It's usually not the breads themselves that contribute so many calories to our diets, but the butter, frostings, and jellies we add to them. Sugar-coated dry cereals don't really count as grain foods because their chief ingredient is sugar. Substituting grain foods for meat, sugar, and fats can also save money. Baking your own bread seems to make grains more appetizing, although it doesn't seem to be part of the normal kitchen routine anymore. Since grains have become such a big part of my family's diet, we invested in a small mill to grind our own wheat and rye flour and corn meal, but for most people, its cost isn't justifiable.

Even though drastic diet changes are not easily accepted (especially by young children), healthful foods can cleverly be worked into a diet over a period of time. More vegetables could be served with meals and for snacks and fewer sugar treats made available.

For snacks after school, children will eat anything that is within reach and doesn't run away. Keep nutritious, tasty snack foods around instead of junk food. Have on hand dry-roasted unsalted peanuts, whole-grain crackers, green pepper, carrot and celery sticks, fresh and dried fruits and juices—without added sugar. Instead of cookies, caramels, or donuts, Ruth gives her children a cup of sunflower seeds to work on at the beginning of a long trip. (Her in-laws have a powerful vacuum.) At our house, I put a bowl of vegetable sticks on the table with dinner. They aren't the first thing eaten, but when we have finished eating and talking and laughing, the vegetables are always gone. Vegetables can be cut up several pounds at a time so that they are readily available in the refrigerator for lunch or snack time. By occasionally serving Chinese-style stir-fried vegetables, you can add a cup per person of crisp, colorful, nutritious vegetables to a meal. If you put forth the effort to grow a garden, you will naturally eat more vegetables—just picture those tasty fresh tomatoes!

More and more in our country, we are turning to convenience foods because we are in a hurry. Much nutrition is lost in their preparation and storage. Next time you reach for a convenience food, stop and ask yourself if you couldn't prepare something more nutritious in the same amount of time. In fifteen minutes, you can have the vegetables chopped for a tasty stew. The soup can cook while you are doing other things, and the leftovers can be refrigerated for a fast lunch. The secret is not to add extra preparation time, but to plan ahead to make better use of the time you do have.

GETTING CHILDREN TO EAT RIGHT

These recommendations may seem sound to you, but you're probably asking yourself, "How do I get my children to eat better foods?" This is the time for reverse psychology. What happens when the doctor prescribes 7-Up and lots of liquids for a sick child? The other kids beg for the same "special" diet. This idea can apply to other foods. "This asparagus is a special grown-up dish I made for Grandpa because it's his favorite." The kids will beg for it. "All right, I'll give you a little taste." Intsead of the parent insisting, the child is asking. After the child has tasted it, he may not like it, and that's fine for now, but he has a mental image of this food being desirable to someone else. If the adults eat reasonably, eventually the children will too. I used to buy a very small bottle of taco sauce for my husband to use on his tacos—it was too hot for the children and it lasted three months. Now everyone has to have the "special" sauce every time we serve burritos or tacos. They eat so much that we now can our own sauce.

Atmospheric conditions nurture the acceptance of foods; therefore, our family has developed three effective rules for mealtime. Because negative attitudes about food are very contagious, the first standing rule is Negative comments cannot be tolerated—if your remarks cause someone else not to eat his food, you must eat all of his portion, too. The second rule simply states, You must taste everything. If, after tasting something, your child doesn't care for it, fine; bread and peanut butter are available. No force, threats, or coaxing are necessary because that's just the way things are. This rule is also effective because it puts the responsibility to eat directly where it belongs—with the child.

Kids are very smart. If they think they can get something more desirable or sweet after the meal, they'll hold out for it. So the third rule is: Nothing to eat later. If the parents are consistent, the children will learn to eat at mealtime. In a positive environment, children will learn to like most foods. Keep in mind, though, that young children and babies have many more taste buds and are very sensitive to strong flavors like tomatoes and seasonings such as curry, onion, or chili powder. Even though you are an adult, there are still probably some foods you don't care for. Understand that your children will have a few dislikes, too. Our two sons have exactly opposite favorites and hates—pizza and burritos. To accommodate them, we haven't totally eliminated either food, and I don't fix two menus in one night. We just rotate menus, and when a hate comes up, that son eats bread and peanut butter—but at the table, with the rest of the family.

MEAL VARIETY

Mary Monotony said she feeds her family the same seven meals every week: roast on Sunday, then tacos, spaghetti, meat loaf, macaroni and cheese, hamburgers, and tuna casserole. Her habits are not unusual. Most families use ten basic menus 80 percent of the time. What could Mary do to get more variety? She could vary the ingredients for spaghetti and serve pizza. The hamburger from the meat loaf might be mixed with corn meal to make tamale pie. Variety doesn't need to cost more in preparation time or money, it just takes thought. To overcome that "what shall I fix for dinner" problem, I began keeping a list of main dishes we liked in my planning notebook—including economy and quick meals; summer and winter ideas. We cook lots of soup and bake many kinds of breads, meats, and vegetables in the winter, but when it is hot, we serve more salads and grilled meals. The menu list helps me recall our favorite dishes from last year, which I tend to forget.

There are several ways to broaden your cooking abilities, but the "see and do" method is best for me. I wanted to learn to cook our favorite Mexican food—cheese enchiladas—but the directions sounded as though it would take four pans and two hours to prepare. My mother-in-law kept telling me it was so simple: "All you have to do is make a chili-powder gravy and roll cheese and onions in corn tortillas"—but it wasn't until after I had watched her that I could make them. Since then, my friends and family have taught me to make flour tortillas, egg noodles, and Chinese eggrolls; to cut up a chicken; to preserve food; and to decorate cakes. To perk up your cooking, watch for notices of cooking demonstrations and classes in your area, or trade skills with a friend. Once you have learned a cooking technique, there are many related recipes that you can make without help. For instance, the procedure used in bread making is also used in making coffee cakes, rolls, donuts, and pretzels.

Families like variety, but not too much of it. I try a brand-new idea only once or twice a month and have twenty-eight old favorites the rest of the time. I make a grocery list as I am planning the meals. This menu list is then posted on the refrigerator to remind us of what we have left in the house to cook. The experience of taking time to plan the meals a week or more ahead will help you add variety. Some meal planners can get by with just listing the main dishes, buying plenty of vegetables and salad ingredients, and then putting them together as the days go by. Others will want to fill in the full menu on a calendar-type chart to get the complete meal picture. Families with special diet requirements for weight, diabetes, heart conditions, and allergies will find meal planning helps add variety, even with their limited food list.

To add to the natural desirability of food, serve it attractively and give it an interesting name. Yankee-Doodle-Beef sounds better than macaroni and tomato casserole. In fact, I don't even say the word "casserole" in front of my children. In a Chinese cooking class, I learned how to strip the outer layer off the stem of broccoli and then thinly slice it for stir-frying. The slices looked just like the silhouette of a turtle, so I named it Chinese Turtles (broccoli stems) and Trees (broccoli tops). They loved it, and we eat it often.

THE SIMPLIFIED MEAL PATTERN

School children are taught a rhyme about the basic food groups by the National Dairy Council: "One for my muscles, two for glow, three to make ready and four to grow." A meal pattern is a simple way to help you judge whether your menus comprise all the basic food groups and help the children grow. The simplest, surest meal pattern to follow for a good daily balance of nutrients is to select foods from each of the four basic food groups: fruits and vegetables, protein foods, grain products, and dairy products. Don't be fooled by thinking you are getting all the nutrients you need by taking a multiple vitamin; there is no one miracle vitamin or miracle food. About fifty nutrients, including water, are needed *daily* for optimum health. You don't have to remember to count them, because they are all found in the basic four food groups. Don't be like the young man who said, "I don't worry about getting the right foods every day; I eat a balanced week." But does he? Is he confusing his metabolism with great amounts of sugar one day and all protein the next? Is he getting the daily requirements of vitamins and minerals by skipping vegetables and grains several days in a row? Is he getting the most possible usable protein by eating complementary protein foods at the same meal, e.g., 1¼ ounces of cheese, when served with ¾ cup cooked rice, yields 20 percent more usable protein than when it is served alone. He could be sure if he ate a wider variety of foods every day.

Each meal should contain one food from each of the four basic food groups. Often several of the food types, such as protein and grains, will be mixed together (as in a peanut-butter sandwich or spaghetti with meatballs). But no matter if you are young or old, if you mentally note whether you have foods from each unit in that meal, your diet will be quite well balanced. Adults don't need the dairy product unit as often as children, and naturally you'll try to choose one fruit every day which is high in vitamin C. If dinner is your biggest meal, you'll probably have two types of food then from the fruit and vegetable unit. Because you actually need only two servings of protein a day, you can miss one protein food at one meal during the day.

Picture the meal pattern as you are preparing a meal to check for a vacancy. Our culture usually has more fruits for breakfast and lunch and more vegetables for dinner, but don't be afraid to change them around. Vary the colors, textures, and temperatures of your meals. Children eat for taste and looks, but the cook thinks of economy and nutrition. Colors, textures, and temperatures can be coordinated with a little extra planning, especially at the beginning of your efforts to improve nutrition.

COMPLEMENTARY PROTEINS

I must add one more point about nutrition. A hundred years ago, as we looked around the world and witnessed deformity and starvation, the cause was diagnosed as malnutrition from not eating enough complete protein. (A complete protein food is one that contains the ten basic amino acids that the body can't manufacture by itself for bodybuilding.) We knew that animal proteins had all the essential amino acids, so we began emphasizing eating lots of meat to avoid the sicknesses of the rest of the world.

But eating meat is not the only way to get enough complete protein. In fact, you can eliminate meats entirely if you know how to serve complementary foods together. If we were collating ten stacks of papers and one pile ran out, the rest of the collated packets would be incomplete. The body is much the same; it can only use complete sets of protein. The leftover amino acids will simply be used for energy rather than tissue building. If you eat wheat, which is low in essential lysine, with beans, which are high in lysine, you actually get more usable protein than if you ate the two foods separately. This is why the Mexicans survived for centuries by supplementing beans with corn, and why the Orientals survived on rice and beans. Sending a peanut-butter or cheese sandwich in a lunchbox provides a complete protein because the nutrients in the peanuts or cheese complement the nutrients in the wheat of the bread. Milk will complement pancakes or cereal. Rice and milk pudding, macaroni and cheese, bean soup and cornbread are all complementary-protein dishes. The following chart shows the complementary triangle formed between grains, dairy products, and legumes.

Practical Application:
Commit yourself to making menus for one month. Then evaluate:

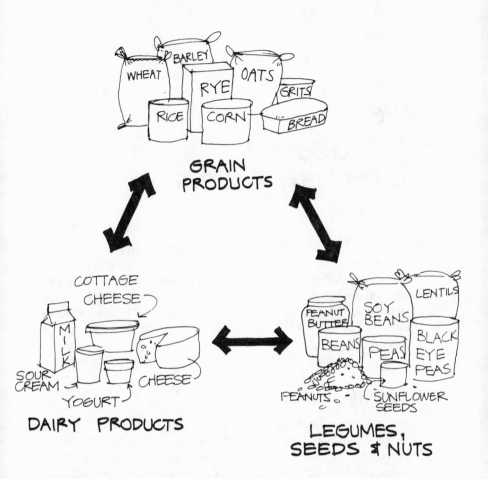

Food triangle. When eaten together at the same meal, foods from any two of these three groups complement each other and actually give more usable protein than if the two foods were eaten separately.

_____Have our meals been more nutritious?
_____Did I spend more or less money on food?
_____Was the meal preparation easier?
_____Were the meals served on time more often?
_____With this plan, did we eat out more or less?
_____Was more time spent cooking?
_____Did this plan save extra trips to the grocery store?
_____Did we eat a wider variety of meals?

*16
How to Spend Fewer Food Dollars

Cost alone is not an indication of a good meal. Nutritional value, color, texture, and flavor all help determine the desirability of food. A vegetarian steak can be nutritious but might be rejected at mealtime as too unfamiliar or "tasting funny." Your challenge is to provide meals that are eaten and enjoyed, that provide the necessary nutritional value, and that keep you within a reasonable food budget.

ALLOCATING THE FOOD BUDGET

You could buy everything as it is needed every day at the store, but experience proves that this is costly and time consuming. The more trips you make to the store, the more you buy from those tempting displays. First decide how much money you will spend for food each month, and then decide what method of dividing your food dollars works best for your needs.

Shopping with a set amount of cash is a method that seems to work for those who buy what looks good on impulse. It seems so much easier to put back convenience foods and unnecessary goodies when you can see how much money they will actually take. If you use this method, take with you only the amount of *cash* you intend to spend. Some of us need that extra strength a limit gives.

Money-by-the-day means designating a specific amount of money, say $5.40, for food each day, and then planning menus within that amount. Each meal has a price; breakfast: $.75; lunch: $1.50; and dinner: $4.25. Calculating how much each item is costing is a revealing exercise that will help you cut food costs even if you don't use this plan. If you take the time to figure the cost of the basic staples, you can know that you spent 86¢ to bake a batch of bread or that dinner cost $2.68. After the menus are planned within their cost allotment, you can make a shopping list. After you've been doing this for a while, the planning won't take as long because you will have built a nice repertoire of menus within your budget.

The fifth method is another way to divide the food dollar.

milk and milk products	one-fifth
meat, fish, poultry, eggs	one-fifth
fruits and vegetables	one-fifth
breads and cereals	one-fifth
other foods (fats, sugar)	one-fifth

If you have a small food budget, you may spend more on grain and legume foods and less on meat in this method. By combining low-cost starch foods such as noodles, potatoes, rice, and beans with meats, fish, cheese, and vegetables, you'll have tasty meals.

Budgeting by category is a variation of the money-by-the-day method. The following figures are monthly allocations:

breakfasts	$15
lunches	$15
dinners	$60
paper and cleaning products	$15
staples and bulk food	$35
fresh items, midway	
in pay period	$10
meat from freezer	$25
	$175 per month total

Having flour, shortening, sugar, eggs, and salt on hand from the staples allotment, you could have pancakes, waffles, muffins, or bread instead of toast for breakfast. The allotted $15 for breakfast would go for fruit, juices, syrup, and cereals—all those extra items not available from staples or fruits canned in the fall. You will see right away that you won't get much the rest of the month if you spend $3 on bacon, even if you could stretch it for several meals.

Having a big roast one night will cost more than your $2 allotment for each evening meal, but if you have some left for inexpensive soups and sandwiches, it may equalize the cost per meal for the month. Try calculating and recording the cost of your meals for several weeks or a month—you'll probably be surprised at how well this works to cut your food bill.

Buying food (especially fruits and vegetables) when it is in season and in larger quantities helps cut the yearly cost. In the summer, we process fruits and vegetables, and in the fall, we stock up on grains. When fresh produce is very expensive in the spring, we eat our bottled fruits and vegetables. In the winter, I buy nuts and honey. Some families find it economical to buy whole sides of beef or pork at one time. This is feasible only if you have a large freezer, but make sure that you find a butcher you can trust or who will let you inspect the meat before you purchase it.

Setting aside a few dollars to buy a little extra food each month will save you money and protect your family. You save two ways: if you buy four extra cans of evaporated milk and the price is up three cents next month, you have saved 12¢, almost 7 percent of the cost of the milk. Also, if you buy in larger quantities, you may save by getting a price break. For example, a bulk purchase of fifty pounds of rolled oats may cost $9.50. If you bought the same fifty pounds in five-pound cartons, it would cost you nearly $20, and for individual serving packets, it could cost $50. You will need to use common sense in your "extended" buying, taking into consideration your storage space and circumstances.

Buying ahead is a practical type of insurance. Everyone should keep on hand enough food for a two-week emergency. Hundreds of things could happen—a crippling snowstorm, a power blackout, an illness, or a labor strike could temporarily cut off your food sources. A two-week "cushion" takes a small amount of space and some planning ahead.

I shop once a month because we get paid that way, and I go back mid-month for fresh salad items and fruit. I've become very proficient in anticipating our buying needs. For most people, it would be more practical to shop twice a month, but I learned to make this plan work for me. If I don't shop at the first of the month when we have money, there is too much month left when the money is gone. We can put off most purchases, but not eating.

GETTING MORE FOR LESS–FORTY WAYS TO CUT THE FOOD BUDGET

As freshmen in college, each of my five roommates and I put in $4 a week for food (the good old days). Our combined food budget would provide for milk, simple breakfasts and lunches, and all dinners, including one with company. As sophomores, living with five different roommates, we each put in $6 a week. This didn't include milk, breakfast, lunch, or company. One girl still had to add more money from her own pocket because she couldn't cook for a week for six on $36. *Why?* Looking for the answer to that question was the beginning of my search for the reasons that some cooks can prepare wholesome meals within a reasonable budget.

Each of the following ideas could save you money. No one will want to use all of them, because our circumstances and tastes in food are different. Check the ones you use or would like to try.

	We will try this.	This could be modified to work for us.
1. Determine food-budget limits before shopping.	_____	_____
2. Pay cash for groceries.	_____	_____
3. Go shopping only *once* during each pay period.	_____	_____
4. Buy and maintain a freezer.	_____	_____
5. Prepare a list *before* shopping, considering seasonal products, specials, and your needs determined from recipes and food cupboards.	_____	_____
6. While you plan menus, make the shopping list.	_____	_____
7. Estimate costs on grocery list. Keep within your budget.	_____	_____
8. Don't go shopping when you are sick, hungry, depressed, or angry.	_____	_____

	We will try this.	This could be modified to work for us.
9. Market early or late to avoid crowds.	_____	_____
10. Leave children and spouse at home.	_____	_____
11. Use the unit-pricing information that most stores provide.	_____	_____
12. Avoid convenience and processed foods.	_____	_____
13. Drink only powdered milk.	_____	_____
14. Keep basic baking staples on hand so you can make a variety of things without returning to the store.	_____	_____
15. Make bread, rolls, stuffing, and croutons at home.	_____	_____
16. Avoid buying prepared desserts and snacks.	_____	_____
17. Figure the cost per serving or cost per meal to see where the money really goes.	_____	_____
18. Buy in larger quantities if you have storage space.	_____	_____
19. Check newspapers and magazines for coupons for items you normally buy.	_____	_____
20. Transfer anything you can't find or afford to a new list.	_____	_____
21. Eat less meat. Extend protein with rice, noodles, wheat or other grains. Mix meat with texturized vegetable protein. Use milk, grains or beans (see chart on page 137) as protein complements to insure full protein nutrition.	_____	_____

	We will try this.	This could be modified to work for us.
22. Cut down or eliminate potato chips and other crunchy, salty snacks.	_____	_____
23. Cut down or eliminate soft drinks and bottled water.	_____	_____
24. Don't buy bacon.	_____	_____
25. Buy only what's on your list; avoid all impulse buying.	_____	_____
26. If you decide to buy an unplanned special, eliminate another item of equal value on the list.	_____	_____
27. Compare frozen, fresh, and canned vegetables for best value.	_____	_____
28. Save money by buying whole chickens, sides of beef, and wheels of cheese. Cut and wrap for your needs.	_____	_____
29. Try buying store-brand products or generic items.	_____	_____
30. Use leftovers. Save gravy, vegetables, and meat in large freezer containers for "end-of-the-month soup."	_____	_____
31. Dehydrate, can, or freeze fruits and vegetables.	_____	_____
32. If you go hunting, use the game meat.	_____	_____
33. Rather than serving meals family style, try dishing up individual portions on plates.	_____	_____
34. Discourage between-meal snacks.	_____	_____

	We will try this.	This could be modified to work for us.
35. Don't serve desserts every day.	_____	_____
36. Make your own cakes, pancakes, and cookies. Put together your own mixes.	_____	_____
37. Grow a garden (the cheapest way to get freshest foods)!	_____	_____
38. Shop at a co-op or warehouse or join a buying club.	_____	_____
39. Buy food from farm stands or farmers' markets (check newspaper ads).	_____	_____
40. Take food from home with you on drives, to the movies, on picnics.	_____	_____

*17
How to Cure "I Want-itis"

Shopping centers make most of their money from Friday night and weekend shoppers who buy on impulse. (Buying on impulse means seeing and buying something you hadn't planned on buying.) These weekend spenders are telling themselves, "You work hard all week; you deserve a reward," and so they buy. It is so hard to get control of our spending because we have so many needs, hopes, and ambitions.

Every day when I am working, I think of equipment or furnishings that would make work easier or things look nicer. I bet I could easily spend $200 a day. When I am working in the yard, it is poplar trees and tomato cages that I want, but at the same time, the workshop needs a power drill and sander. (I could also use a full-time handyman to take care of the remodeling.) This "I want-itis" can consume our lives and make us unhappy. We need to learn to be content with what we have and the rate at which we can accumulate more things. To help get control of these desires and whims, consider the following suggestions.

Stay out of stores. If we were to go to the shopping mall today, we would find a bargain we truly needed. By staying home, we won't even know about it. Have you noticed that most rural families maintain a happy life without all the gadgets and conveniences that city homes have? They aren't exposed to the alluring array, and they learn to live simply. You can avoid temptation by staying out of the stores.

Compare yourself to your ancestors. Did they need it? What quality of life did they have without it? I don't want to go back to outhouses and cold water, but it is possible to live a good life without an electric can opener or a massage shower head. Poverty can be a state of mind rather than a situation. I'm not saying we need to deprive ourselves of everything—just that we need to get control of how we spend our money. Continue asking yourself these questions before you buy.

Ask yourself, "Is this item important to my future?" Sunglasses? Record player? If it isn't essential, perhaps you can wait a little longer. You need to ask yourself many questions to get control of this "I want-itis" disease. How much of my life, work, and time is this item worth? Several years ago, I wanted a dehydrator for drying fruits and vegetables. I looked over all the models, I planned and calculated, but just couldn't come up with the $135. The only possible way to get one was to take on some outside work. My time was already completely obligated with family, including a nine-month-old baby. When I evaluated what part of my life I would have to give up for a dehydrator, I decided to do without.

Keep an I Want List in your planning notebook. When money is available, you can choose from the list what you want most, not just what you happen to want today or what you see now. Writing it down frees your mind but keeps the thought.

Consider how much it will cost to maintain it. We couldn't accept the gift of a pipe organ in our new church building because of the high cost of maintenance. What is your time worth? Everything has its care price. A new end table is one more thing to dust and polish. A plant needs watering, feeding, spading, and a monthly shower. We continue taking more into our lives, each requiring a few more moments, until we are slaves to our belongings. Does the pleasure of owning this item outweigh its care price?

Consider how well you take care of what you have. A person who can't keep up with the dishes and dandelions isn't ready for an untrained puppy. Continue asking yourself where you will put it. "Oh, but I want it so much, I'll find a place for it." Watch out—you'll overfill the house. "Do I use what I have?" How often have you really wanted something, then when you got it, didn't use it? Will this be another of those shelf hogs?

Ask yourself, "What else can I use or do instead?" After accepting that I couldn't buy a dehydrator, I went to a demonstration on food drying and learned it could be done in the oven. My husband and I spent an hour making four screen racks for the oven. That season we dried every fruit and vegetable we could and found we didn't care for the dried vegetables. In the end, I didn't need the dehydrator after all.

Be inventive. Whenever we want something, our first impulse is to go get it. Necessity can be the mother of invention. Many times something else will do just as well if we use our imagination. One day when I didn't have time to iron the linen tablecloth, I wanted to buy a new no-iron cloth, but it was the end of the month and there was no money. Instead I tried using a large piece of polyester-knit material from my sewing closet. It worked so well and cost so little that the linen cloth is still in the "inactive" storage closet. Our neighbor used clamp-on ice shoes to aerate his lawn. You can be imaginative; give it a try.

Set money limits before going shopping. "I'll find a nice gift for less than $10." A gift is only a token. Forget the idea that the monetary value of a gift has to equal the depth of your love, and you won't be tempted to buy something on impulse that costs too much. Avoid impulse buying by planning and comparing. If you do comparison shopping, you will know a good bargain when you see it. Whenever a salesperson tells you that this is the last chance to buy, it probably isn't. Since you can't have everything, choose what you can have with care.

Do it yourself. Ben Franklin said, "A penny saved is a penny earned," but now a penny saved is worth *twice* as much as a penny earned. Suppose you can fix your own washing machine, for which the bill would have been $69. To hand out that much spendable income a worker might have had to earn $130 gross salary (it's not unusual for a worker to lose half his gross salary to taxes). No, we can't do everything ourselves, but nowadays, it literally pays to be handy.

After expenses, the working wife is the poorest-paid laborer in our country. "A typical working wife actually nets in a range of 10 to 30 percent of the pay dollar after counting all the costs of working" (taxes, child care, clothing, transportation, and quick foods), says Colein Hefferan, professor of family finances at Pennsylvania State University. If the wife improves her home skills and economizes, it can become more profitable for her to stay at home and save than to go to work and earn. (Certainly, the woman's desires must be considered.) A number of years ago, a mother showed me a lovely spring wardrobe she had just bought at half-price for her two very young daughters for only $120. That's more than I was spending on clothes for myself and four children in a whole year. For my friend to have $120 spendable income, according to Colein Hefferan's statistics, she probably had to earn $360, almost twenty 8-hour workdays (assuming she earned the minimum wage of $2.25 and paid standard taxes and working expenses). At home, I could have created an equivalent wardrobe in 18 hours and for $25.

Plan a budget and use it. You'll be surprised at how much money you can save simply by keeping a monthly (or weekly) budget book in which you record all your expenditures—from the big outlays of cash for rent or mortgage and utilities, to the daily expenditures for such things as newspapers, chewing gum, bus fare, and cigarettes.

There are many good budget books on the market that can help you project your expenditures, allocate your available funds, and keep track of actual purchases. The trick to using these books successfuly, that is, to saving money, is to be absolutely honest and faithful in recording *all* expenditures (it becomes easier to pass up an impulse item when you know that when you get home, you'll have to record the purchase in your budget book).

Practical Application:

Begin your Want Lists for personal and household items. Review your purchases over the last few months and determine how many of them were made by impulse. If you are a victim of impulse, you may need to take up bowling on Friday night as a substitute activity to keep you out of the stores.

SIX

Problem Solving

*18
How to Solve Special Problems

Besides the principles and habits for the home we have already covered, there are four more specific home issues we need to discuss: (1) conquering the dishes, (2) licking the laundry, (3) overcoming the mending, and (4) getting your husband/wife/children to go along with the system. Problems in these areas are very common because they are part of the daily household routine.

After the four special problems comes an explanation of the problem-solving process, with a dozen examples so you can work out solutions to your own special household problems.

CONQUERING THE DISHES

Were you born with self-control? If not, you probably have trouble with the dishes and kitchen cleanup. There is hope, because self-control can be developed. Give yourself a fighting chance in the kitchen by clearing off the counters and work areas before beginning any kitchen job. Don't try to fix dinner over the breakfast mess. You can give yourself a head start by filling the sink with hot soapy water so you can quickly wash up utensils, bowls, and pans as you use them (this is an especially good trick if you have an apartment or home with a small kitchen).

Think of the cleanup as part of the meal, just like the preparation or eating. I recall as a child dreading the day it was my turn to do the dishes because it took me two hours. Whenever I could, I would con my dad into helping because he could do them so fast. If the family immediately cleans off the table and washes the dishes together, no one has to face that long ordeal and all are free to take care of other responsibilities or play.

Suppose the cook has helped with the dishes by washing or soaking the equipment used in preparation. Wash the rest of the dishes in this order: glassware, silverware, plates and bowls, serving pieces, utensils, and pots and pans. Rinse everything in very hot water and drain dry (life is too short to dry dishes!). Tackle one sinkful at a time, pat yourself on the back, and do another sinkful until everything is finished.

If the kitchen is in such a mess that you don't know where to begin, start by clearing a spot for the clean dishes, then clear off the other tables and counters, one at a time, either clockwise or counterclockwise, depending on your kitchen arrangement. If you have an automatic dishwasher, rinse off the food particles and store the dishes inside the washer until you have enough to justify running a full cycle. You will probably still have some utensils, pans, or plastic containers that cannot go into the dishwasher. Take care of them right away. If the washing is delayed, at least stack the dishes near the sink to clear the table and the counters.

Use a clean dishcloth and towel each day. Food particles that are on the cloth and towel will sour and spoil. Don't recontaminate everything. Notice the lift a clean, new dishcloth gives as you wipe up the drainboard and counters—it almost makes the job a pleasure.

Since dishes have to be washed so often, learn to do it quickly. "Let's see how much of the kitchen we can get clean in fifteen minutes." If you need to, create an incentive. "After I finish the dishes, I'll take a hot bath." As you pass the kitchen, enjoy the clean counters because they show that you're a successful housekeeper.

LICKING THE LAUNDRY PROBLEM

No wonder the laundry is such a big job. The average family of four will have 224 items of clothing to wash in a week (not including linens), and each article is handled at least six times before it gets back into the closet. If this clean clothing isn't promptly put away, it becomes clutter. Let's look into several homes and see how these home managers have conquered their laundry.

Jean is a mother of five children who does all the laundry in one day; Marilyn, mother of eight, sets aside two days a week to wash; Greg, as a bachelor, does his laundry every other weekend; and Faye, mother of three, washes one or two loads a day. They have each found a way to have the clothes clean and in place without having piles of dirty or clean laundry cluttering the home. Keeping up with the laundry actually saves money, because fewer clothes are needed. If we tagged a shirt and followed it through the delays in an unorganized household that washes, folds, irons, and delivers clothing sporadically, we would see that it may take seventeen days for the shirt to get back in the closet. You will notice that such a family makes many trips to the washroom to retrieve clothing.

To save time, the first rule for laundry control is to *do as much laundry at once as possible,* without overworking the washing machine or yourself. Your circumstances and the physical features of your home will affect your type of system. If everyone in your household wears jeans or casual clothes, your technique will be different from that of the family in which everyone dresses professionally for work. Small children in diapers and spouses who are auto mechanics cause special laundry problems.

Faye, mother of three, works full-time and found it best to wash two batches a day. She has four bins on wheels under the folding table

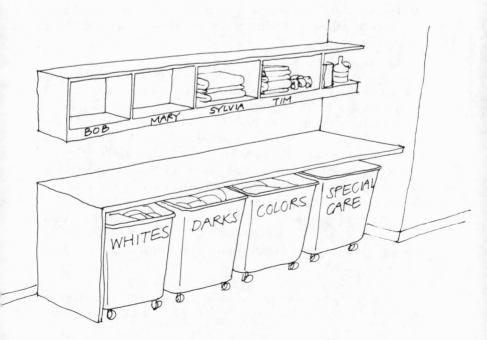

in her laundry room to separate the soiled clothing (see page 153). This helps her avoid "overwashing" or mixing wrong articles together just to get enough for a full load. As the family members take their soiled clothing to the wash area, they put each item in the appropriate bin. Boxes or baskets on shelves (see illustration, page 86), could also work. Faye has labeled the bins: dark, white, colored, and special care. Before she goes to work, she loads and starts the washer with a batch of clothes from the bin that has enough for a load. When she gets home, she dries the first load while a second batch is washing. On Wednesday, her day off, she washes the special-care batch so they can be pressed and immediately put away. Faye has this system so organized that anyone can step in occasionally and take over the washing.

Marilyn, mother of eight, never felt caught up until she switched to Tuesday-Thursday wash days. This way she didn't have to spend every day in the laundry room. With four little boys in elementary school, it was financially impossible to have enough jeans to get through the week. By washing twice, the boys could have the same jeans clean twice in a week. Marilyn separates the clothing into piles on Tuesday and washes four or five batches as she's cleaning house. On Thursday, she schedules an hour to press the shirts and dresses right after they are pulled from the dryer, making them ready for the weekend.

Greg, a construction worker, found that loading up the dirty clothing and going to the Laundromat took almost the same amount of time whether he was washing three or six loads, so he decided to buy a few more clothes and not wash as often. Greg wisely keeps the soiled clothing in two duffle bags so the dirt from his work clothes doesn't ruin his nicer things. A single person such as Greg, or even a couple, has more flexibility than a family when it comes to washing. They can wash every two or three weeks when they run out of clothing. For them, maintaining a washing machine at home may be just a matter of convenience, while washing at a Laundromat would actually cost less. But a family deals with such a large amount of clothing that an organized laundry procedure with a washer and dryer at home are almost essential.

Jean, mother of five, wanted to bunch all the washing together on one day to be free for other things the rest of the week. Although she does the baby's diapers and linens on other weekdays as she is working in various rooms, the family clothing is all washed and put away in one day. The first step in setting up this procedure was to make sure everyone had enough clothes to last seven days, necessitating the purchase of a few more socks and pairs of underwear and catching up on the mending. Actually, Jean found that her family needed fewer clothes when she was consistent about washing on the same day each week.

Each family member should have a "best" outfit, two or three outfits of clothes left from last year, another for play or work, and three or four new things bought throughout the year making a total of seven outfits—enough for the week. A few hand-me-downs also help fill in. By having each skirt or each pair of pants match one blouse or one shirt, you'll need less clothing than if you have a large variety of clothing that matches only one other item.

Jean has a large hamper or wastebasket in each bedroom to hold the soiled clothing until wash day, when the children carry their baskets to the laundry room. This frees her work room for other projects the rest of the week. After the clothing is separated into boxes according to fabric, color, and amount of soil, she mends the necessary items while the first batch is washing. Each new article of clothing is hand washed the first time to see if it fades, rather than risk turning a whole batch of clothes pink, gray, or blue. Jean stays close to the washer and dryer, hanging, folding, and pressing most of the day. She puts all the clean clothes away in one day. What a boost to the pickup process!

Some people never have any ironing to do and some others never get theirs done. If you prefer crisp, ironed shirts, ask yourself, when will it be done? Schedule your washing when you can include the ironing. One woman said, "If my husband doesn't get picky about wanting his favorite shirts, I can go two months without ironing." How many shirts does he have and how big is his closet? Where does she keep them while they are waiting to be ironed? Some families can solve this problem by sending the shirts to a commercial laundry. Others, who must do it at home, prefer having a set time to do the ironing for the week or assign it to another family member. Then it won't be sitting in a basket (getting more wrinkled) or hanging around waiting until there is time or enough items to make the project worthwhile.

Deciding on a system to fold, sort, and put away clean clothing will help you complete the chore. Some families wash by room, a system in which all clothes in a load come from the same room. The disadvantage of this method is that all these articles may not belong together in one batch—brown corduroy jeans should be washed separately from white shirts. It's better to wash two smaller loads and adjust the water level than to mix towels with lingerie, blue denims with permanent press, or diapers with face cloths.

A table for folding is especially helpful near the laundry area. Set up a card table on washday if you can't have a table there permanently. Separate and fold clothes into piles by room or individual. Boxes, baskets, dishpans, or shelves will help you organize. If you don't have room on the wall for permenant shelves or square cubbyholes (like post-office sorting boxes, only larger), use boxes or baskets that can be spread out on wash day and then stacked and put away.

One trick is to color code all the children's clothing so someone else can easily help sort. Each child is assigned a different color. Cut small half-inch squares from scrap fabric (most polyester knits won't ravel or fade) and secure them with a small gold safety pin to the back of each garment (this also helps little ones learn front from back). As an article is passed to another child, it is easy to change the colored tag. To color code socks, run a basting stitch across the toe with embroidery floss.

Now we're ready to discuss putting away these 224 items. Don't start putting away clothing until everything that goes to a specific room has been washed and folded, because making only one trip to each room is part of the efficiency plan. I straighten the drawers as I'm putting away the clean clothes. It has not been successful for me to try to get my children to put their own clean things away. If I do it, I can keep close track of the clothing and get finished without having to nag or wait for the children.

What about unmatched socks? Keep them in a specific area other than on top of the dryer and hope the missing mate will show up next week. After a few weeks, tie the mateless socks together. If the mates still don't show up in another month, consider them lost and toss out the whole bundle or let someone make puppets from them.

Review the clothing as it is folded, making notes of special needs. If an article is worn out or too small, put it away for your next child or put it in the charity basket until you have enough to drop off. This gives a little time for someone to "miss" the article. If they haven't noticed it is gone in two weeks, it's pretty safe to give it away. Save the buttons and zippers if the article isn't good enough for someone else to wear, and use the cloth for rags.

Do we use hand-me-downs? Yes, and we have saved lots of money that way, but be aware of several things: (1) Clothes look worse with age, so save them sparingly; (2) you must be willing to mend or alter the hand-me-downs; (3) don't feel obligated to wear them out. You may feel a necessity to see that your son gets good use out of the shirt you spent $15 on, but look without emotion at a shirt that someone else has given you; and (4) (perhaps the most important rule of all) don't collect too many hand-me-downs. If you get more than you need, give them away.

After all the clothes are washed, folded, and put away, wipe off the machines, sweep the floor, and enjoy that beautiful *finished* feeling for a whole week.

OVERCOMING THE MENDING

You are not alone if you have mending headaches. I found in a recent home problem survey that 74 percent of the homes had problems getting their mending caught up—just like death and taxes, it's always with us. The first secret of handling the mending problem is to have a time set aside *each week* to mend those things that were damaged in the last seven days. There aren't as many as you might think. One family of seven only has four or five articles to mend each week, but oh, what a mountain if they were saved up for several months. Right now, decide when you will do this week's mending. One woman does it during the first half-hour on laundry day while the first batch is washing. Another good time is when you are watching TV.

The second secret is to have on hand the materials and equipment necessary to mend—thread in many colors, elastic, scraps of fabric, patches (plain or fancy, iron- or sew-on), buttons, seam ripper, and sewing machine (not necessary, but helpful) with a good supply of bobbins. You'd be surprised how many people don't mend because they hate to wind bobbins. On most machines, you can wind the next color bobbin *while* you sew by not loosening the hand wheel.

"I'm behind, how do I catch up?" Go through the mending stack and sort out those clothes that are not worth fixing and those that don't fit anymore. Get rid of the ones that would not be worn even if mended. Put them in grocery bags in the car and drop them off at a charity stop the next time you go out. (Charity retail stores sell rags to painters or to recycling factories.) Now you have probably eliminated more than half of the mending stack. One reason you didn't get to the mending was that many of these clothes were not drastically needed.

Now make it a special goal to get what's left of your mending stack caught up. You have already set aside a time to do the weekly mending. Now, at least, you won't get any further behind. Make a time to work on the rest of the mending. If you repaired two more articles than were torn each week during mending time, eventually you would be caught up. Or, if you want faster progress, set aside a specific afternoon each week to work on the mending mountain until it is gone. Then stay caught up. During seasonal changes when we get out a different set of clothes, I find I need to take a day or two to make the necessary alterations. One money-saving bonus of keeping up with the mending is that you don't need as many clothes.

The third secret to conquering the mending is to learn how to mend. Most mending falls into very simple categories if it is done in the beginning. Remember, in all mending and alterations, ask yourself, if this garment is mended, is it worth the time it will take to fix it? Will fixing it extend its wear beyond this season?

Seam Restitching
Most mending and repairs are on the seams. Simply restitch the seam with matching thread. Be generous in overlapping the original stitching to prevent the chain stitching from pulling out.

Holes in Knits
Whether a hole is created from a broken thread or nibbled by a pet gerbil, it can be repaired with a needle and thread. Using a single thread and putting the knot on the wrong side of the garment, catch the little loops before they run and secure them by sewing back and forth across the hole. This is where a stitch in time can save the garment. Few people darn socks anymore because the new fabric blends wear until the whole sock is worn out, but if a stitch should

come loose in a good pair of socks, catching the loop before it runs may be worth the effort.

Knee Patches for Jeans

Keep on hand a few scraps of heavy fabric to be sewn underneath the hole for reinforcement. Using a matching color of thread, stitch back and forth over the hole many times, going far enough into the good fabric to hold it securely. This can be done by hand or with a free-arm-model sewing machine. If you delight in a fancy patch, put one over the stitching on the right side of the fabric.

Hems

Don't be afraid to take up or let down hems. Modern fabric blends usually won't show a hem change if they are sprayed with vinegar-water and pressed. Letting down a girl's dress to a very small hem may give it enough length to finish out the season. Consider a fancy machine stitch or a trim such as lace or rickrack to cover the hem crease if it shows.

Cutoffs

Cutting off long sleeves gives a little more wear from a shirt. The "high-water" pants from last season can be cut off for summer shorts, or a long dress can be shortened to knee length.

Buttons

Restitch a loose button before you lose it and save a headache later when you have to match it. Take buttons off old clothes that aren't good enough for wearing and keep them for replacements.

Zippers

Zippers take a little more sewing skill to replace, but if the garment is worth an hour of your time, then make the effort. Not having a sewing machine is not a good excuse here, since zippers can be put in by hand (very expensive clothing has hand-sewn zippers). Putting a new zipper in a pair of wearable pants might take only twenty minutes. Putting a new zipper in a coat takes an hour but may give you another twenty dollars' worth of wear. Is that a fair exchange?

Make a scrap book or box in which you keep an extra square of material from each article you've made in case it is needed for a repair job. One family that keeps such a book enjoys looking back at the fabrics that their clothes were made from. Later, these blocks could be used to make a memory quilt.

HOW CAN I GET HIM/HER TO GO ALONG WITH THE SYSTEM?

What can I do about a spouse who seems to be working against me instead of with me? How do I get our children to be tidier when this thoughtlessness is such a bad example?" Disagreement over the standard level of housekeeping affects both sexes, no matter who is in charge of the home care.

What can those of us with this problem do? First, we must accept people as they are. Quit trying to change them, and they are more likely to change themselves. You can only change yourself and your own attitude. When you increase your efforts to improve and get organized, most partners catch the spirit and cooperate.

Positive comments will get far better results than negative nagging and hinting. Of course, you can't be as gushy with praise as you would with a three-year-old ("You did such a nice job straightening up your desk"), but positive motivation is very effective. Your partner is a grown-up adult who resents hints such as "I wish someone would clean this room." Talk to your spouse in a straightforward, specific manner. "Will you vacuum the floor today?" When you come right out and ask, you may get a no, or you might get a definite commitment. Then, after the floor has been vacuumed, acknowledging it in a positive way increases the chances of more cooperation in the future.

Understand your relationships. Because husband-wife housekeeping problems are a very touchy business, it may help to realize that the relationship between wife and husband and the relationship between child and parent are entirely different. A wife with a problem husband could look at it this way: "My husband is my partner. My husband's parents were responsible for training him, but now, as his wife, it is not my job to retrain him. Instead, as two business partners, we want to work out problems together with good communication. I will explain to him what I am trying to do and ask for his help and support. Although I am not in charge of retraining my husband, as a parent, I am now responsible to train my children. When they throw their father's faults up to me, I will explain these differences in our relationships and carry on with their training." A father might use the same approach in helping the child understand a mother's weaknesses.

Stop and look for the causes. Richard, who was dissatisfied with his wife's housekeeping, found the cause to be that his wife had more to do than she could handle because the major share of managing twenty-one apartments fell to her: cleaning, collecting rent, showing apartments, and handling complaints. Her housekeeping was greatly improved when they moved to a smaller unit. In another case, LeeAnn was discouraged about waiting for her husband to fix the house. He took down her kitchen cabinets, anticipating remodeling the kitchen, but he hadn't gotten back to it in two years. She tried to be very patient, but had only two feet of counter space and one cupboard. When she analyzed the problem, she realized he didn't have the time or energy for remodeling. He was working an eight-hour job and carrying a full load at school. They decided to leave the restoration of the old home to someone else and traded it for one that was already finished. They found the cause—he was too busy—they accepted it, and chose one of the alternatives.

Define the responsibilities. One nice thing about being a couple is that the work of running the home corporation is shared. Some couples decide to divide up all the responsibilities—both work outside the home, both clean the house, and both care for the children. But statistics show this is still more of an ideal than a reality. Other couples stick to the more traditional division, in which the man earns the money while the woman cares for the home and children. One pioneer couple I read about several years ago, broke from the traditional roles: Grandma killed the rattlesnakes and Grandpa scrubbed the floors. It doesn't matter who does what so much as it matters that the couple has discussed the division of responsibility and has come to specific agreements. To make a relationship work, you must be willing to do more than your share, because from your angle it always looks as if you are doing more than the other person. But take warning. If you do take over your partner's territory, it could be yours for life. You may help, assist, or trade off, but do not take over.

Keep up your part of the bargain. There was once a queen who donned her best clothes and took her court hunting when a crisis was pending. As her subjects saw the royal procession parading for the hunt, they assumed that all must be well, and carried on with their chores instead of panicking. It works the same at home. Like the queen, if the man or woman puts forth extra effort to do his or her own part better when the partner is troubled or depressed, it will lift the other's emotions and give added strength. The work won't be done any better or faster if both partners give up because one person is having trouble with her or his share of the responsibility.

When you or your partner has been away from home for a while, whether on business or on vacation, allow time to acclimatize to the change in environment before facing decisions, home crises, naughty children, undone chores, or social engagements. If one adult has remained at home, he or she can consciously smooth the waters and thus avoid the resentments and arguments that typically ignite at this critical time. (You'll notice that a child returning home from grandma's house, school, or even a birthday party needs this same readjustment time.)

If you have tried all these methods with love, patience, and kindness, and serious problems still remain, perhaps you need outside help. There may be a compassionate friend or family member, a doctor, lawyer, or marriage counselor you can talk with. You may find answers in how-to books or classes or help from church, state, or county social services.

P.S.: There isn't a man or woman in the world who doesn't have at least one fault that bothers her or his partner—just be glad it isn't worse.

*19
The Problem-Solving Process

One very hot day an industrious young boy wanted to earn money to go roller-skating so he decided there would be a market for lemonade. He made a small sign with a pencil, got a box, cups, and pitcher, and set up in the shade of the garage. He waited patiently. At noon he marked down the price. Still no one came. At 3 P.M. he abandoned the project and sadly went inside the house. He felt like a failure, as though no one liked him. Actually it wasn't his personal qualities that were at fault but his marketing techniques. His sign needed to be darker and bigger. He needed to move his box out where he could be seen and to involve his friends in the project.

When you have a problem at home, do you take it as a personal insult? You, too, may have a marketing or managing misfunction. Step out of the emotion and, as a manager, analyze the situation. You have a marvelous computer—your brain—available to aid in setting up a plan. Your computer has already been taking in great amounts of varied data through formal education and daily living. By feeding the problem into your computer, you can obtain a workable solution. In order to properly feed the problem into the computer, you need to take a careful look at the situation.

Identifying the *why* is the first step to a solution. Let's look at Donna's problem. She hated to get up every morning. As she began evaluating *why*, she realized it wasn't because she was tired but because she didn't want to face the dilemma in the kitchen: "What shall I fix for breakfast?" Another woman, Linda, lingered in bed because she dreaded facing last night's dishes. Even though Donna and Linda had the same problem of not wanting to get up, the causes were different, and so will be their solutions. Take time to specify the problem and the *why* by writing them down.

Since your computer doesn't come with a printout feature, you will also need to write down its output. The brain tosses out answers like bubbles coming to the surface—one here, one there, and often only once. After Donna had identified the problem, her brain began sending out possible reasons: She had skimped on buying breakfast ingredients for more expensive dinners; she was tired of the same old things, and so on. Then the output of possible solutions began: Plan ahead, skip breakfast altogether, create a variety. The ideas didn't all come at one sitting; they came in bits and parts. Even if the value of an idea wasn't apparent, Donna recorded each of them.

Donna sought outside information from other computers by watching the food section of the newspaper and discussing it with her friends. She went to a lecture on Making Breakfast Breezy. Then Donna evaluated all the information she had gathered and set specific goals. "I will plan breakfast one week ahead, allot $5 extra to spark up breakfast, and keep a permanent list of breakfast ideas in my planning notebook for reference." Donna followed through on her goals. It became easier for her to crawl out of bed in the morning, and her family's interest in food perked up. She was making progress.

Some problems can be solved in a one-time effort and others are only conquered for today. If your challenge is to find a way to keep the coats from landing on your living-room chair, a row of hooks and a little follow-up may solve the problem. A large set of bucket-and-board shelves (see pages 95-96) might be the answer to organizing storage. But the problem of getting children to do their chores in the morning can't be solved in a day. It will take varying incentives and years of follow-up before the children are self-motivated. Some home problems may be difficult to solve and some can never be solved—only improved. Regardless of the problem, identifying it and setting down specific plans to overcome it is a valuable exercise to help get proper perspective and overview. Habits are overcome a little bit at a time. If you can divide a problem into parts small enough to be solved successfully, you will have the motivation to go on.

Remember to complete the minimum maintenance for the rest of the house before working on a project. You won't feel successful if your house goes to pot while you spend three days cleaning out the garage. Keeping up with the meals, dishes, clothes, and pickup will free you to concentrate on the problem area or project and still come out ahead. Work on one area at a time or it will seem like you have all 300,000 items out at once. Even if you are doing your own moving, for example, you can pack one room at a time rather than the whole house at once.

A home is like a living thing—it is always changing. There will always be problems to be worked on, adjustments to be made. But after you have learned to apply the techniques in this book, your problems will be minimized.

There may be times when a problem is so out of hand that the only solution is a fresh start. Sharon had her children take everything out of their bedrooms except the bed and eight days of clothes until they could keep that much clean. LeeAnn found that moving to a completely finished home was the solution to her husband's unfulfilled promises to finish the house. Jerry scooped the clutter of his house into large garbage bags to get an even start. Bob hauled everything in the garage to the dump and started over.

Most problems are manageable if they are tackled with a systematic approach. Here are the steps to the problem-solving formula. For some reason, they are easier to visualize if written out in chart form. The charts on the following pages show how the problem-solving process has been used to fit varying circumstances. Don't try to solve a whole roomful of problems at once. For instance, one of my students said his problem was the rec room—it was a wreck. The room had too much furniture (three pianos, a sofa, a rocking chair, a desk, and a chair, three bookcases, a sewing cabinet and chair, a drop-leaf sewing table, and an exercise bike) and too many unfinished projects (furniture to be stained, car seats to be upholstered, and a pair of slacks under construction). The desk was piled high and the open sewing machine accumulated junk. This family needed to divide the problems in this room into specific parts (books, coats, desk, magazines, mail, filing, furniture) to be worked on one at a time until the whole room was workable again.

PROBLEM-SOLVING FORMULA

1. Recognize the problem and define it in writing.
2. Determine why it is a problem.
3. Set a goal—what would be the ideal situation.
4. Brainstorm for ideas and write them down.
5. Seek outside information.
6. Make a detailed, specific to-do list that will help you achieve your goal/ideal situation.
7. If the plan doesn't work, find out why. Perhaps the goals need to be modified or changed.

Identify Problem: *I'm always embarrassed to have guests visit my home.*

Why is it a problem?	Goal or Ideal Situation	Brainstorm Possibilities	To-Do List
When guests come, I seem to notice everything that is wrong.	Have those rooms that are visible to guests straight *most* of the time so that when impromptu or invited guests come, we will not be embarrassed.	Never answer the door or invite anyone in.	1. Never make apologies—who needs to deck the halls with their follies?
I would like everything to be perfect.		Set entries and living room as top-priority areas.	2. Pick up living room and entry twice daily—after breakfast and before dinner.
It's always such a job getting everything ready; perhaps I try to do too much.		Keep the visible rooms free of clutter.	3. Allow time several days before invited guests are to arrive to get house straight, concentrating most effort in top-priority areas.
Even though rooms aren't dirty, they are littered—really only 10 minutes away from being neat.		Establish limits for these rooms.	4. Sweep porch and wipe around entry doorways weekly.
		Share pickup responsibility with others.	
		Invite guests more often so I can get more efficient at getting ready.	5. Keep beverages, snacks, and a few quick-meal ingredients on hand if we should like to offer guests something to eat.
		Give each room 10 minutes a day.	
		Set time goal every day to have rooms straight.	6. Meet with household members to set limits on uses

Identify Problem: *The drawer is overflowing with recipes. I must lose 30 hours a year hunting through them.*

Why is it a problem?	Goal or Ideal Situation	Brainstorm Possibilities	To-Do List
Too many recipes.	1. To be able to find the recipe I need quickly and easily.	File recipes.	1. Buy an accordion-style file folder and label with basic food categories.
No time to recopy them.		Quit collecting.	
Many various sizes and textures of papers.	2. To arrange recipes so they take up less room.	Glue recipes on typing paper and put in ring notebook.	2. Go through recipe drawer: a. Throw out recipes we haven't tried or liked in the past year.
	3. To eliminate loss.	Throw out recipes I haven't used.	b. Staple or glue small scraps of paper to 4 x 6 cards so they won't get lost.
		Put recipes in a bigger drawer.	c. File each recipe under general topic.
		Plan to use one new recipe a week.	3. From now on, follow these rules: a. Keep only those recipes we have tried and liked. b. Limit the number of recipes in each type—who needs 9 banana-bread recipes?

Why is it a problem?	Goal or Ideal Situation	Brainstorm Possibilities	To-Do List
			c. After using a recipe, make a note on it telling how it turned out and any recommended changes.
			d. When I get a new recipe, commit myself to a day or time I'll use it.
			4. Try a new recipe the day after weekly shopping is done.

Identify Problem: *I always seem to leave the dirty dishes—the job I hate most—until last.*

Why is it a problem?	Goal or Ideal Situation	Brainstorm Possibilities	To-Do List
No one takes responsibility for emptying the dishwasher.	Dirty dishes will not have to wait for clean dishes in dishwasher to be put away.	Eat off paper plates.	1. Assign and rotate dishwasher duty.
Dirty dishes can often be found stacked on the counter waiting for the dishwasher to be emptied.		Get someone else to do it. Set specific time to do it every day.	2. Display chart showing whose job it is to empty dishwasher.
Washing dirty dishes is a psychological hang-up—I hate it!		Empty dishwasher while talking on the phone. Plan a reward as incentive for every day dishwasher is emptied ahead of schedule.	3. Begin no kitchen project until dishwasher is empty and ready to receive dirty dishes.
We have an inconvenient cupboard arrangement.		Try doing it together as a cooperation task or with teams competing—it's more fun with a friend.	4. Time job and within a week cut the number of minutes it takes by half. 5. If someone will empty dishwasher for me, I'll make that person's bed.

PROBLEM SOLVING

Identify Problem: *Our phone messages always seem to get lost.*

Why is it a problem?	Goal or Ideal Situation	Brainstorm Possibilities	To-Do List
Pencil and paper are never handy.	Phone messages will all be delivered to intended person.	Find a central place to put messages where they will be seen.	1. Buy gadget to hold paper and pencil by phone.
No specific place to put messages.		Keep running list of incoming calls.	2. Immediately put notes and messages on refrigerator with a magnet.
Too many phones.		Buy or rent a phone-message recorder.	3. Give verbal appreciation to the one who carefully takes a message.
Some people don't take responsibility.		Tie pencil to phone.	4. Ask about calls upon arriving home.
Phone answered by people who can't take message.		Hang bulletin board.	5. Discuss need for accurate messages.
		Ask caller to return the call in case the message is not delivered, putting responsibility back on caller.	6. For younger children, conduct practice session of proper way to answer phone, stressing responsibility of passing on any message.

Identify Problem: *Kitchen counters are hardly ever clean. (In this case, there is more than one cause for the problem. Look at each separately for a solution.)*

Why is it a problem?	Goal or Ideal Situation	Brainstorm Possibilities	To-Do List
I haven't been in the habit of doing anything in the kitchen after supper except clearing the table and putting the food away.	Kitchen will be neat the majority of the time.	Put cookbooks away after use.	1. Spend half-hour after dinner cleaning.
Clean dishes, jars, and cookbooks are left sitting on telephone counter.	Meal preparations should go faster because I don't have to hunt things buried in clutter.	Clean up after each project. Take care of mail when it arrives, rather than placing it on phone counter.	2. Spend 15 minutes more each evening going through school papers and mail and cleaning off things accumulated that day.
Counter by phone is the pile-it place for mail, school papers, and books and is clearly visible from the front door. When the clutter gets deep, I am so intimidated by the enormity of clearing it away that it takes a crisis situation for me to drum up the courage to attack it.	I won't be embarrassed or discouraged by a messy kitchen.	Make another place for mail. Clean out cabinets under sink for more storage. Knock out wall and make kitchen larger. Build shelf near back door for schoolbooks, gym clothes, and sack lunches.	3. Buy or build shelves in garage for empty canning jars this summer. 4. In council meeting, discuss putting away snack ingredients after each use. 5. Pot window plants in larger pots and place elsewhere.
Ingredients for snacks are left on counter.		Cut down on number of dishes used.	6. Buy a mail holder and store mail in cupboard.

Why is it a problem?	Goal or Ideal Situation	Brainstorm Possibilities	To-Do List
Too many plants around the sink add to cluttered appearance.		Label shelves for contents so items can be put back in proper space by any cook.	
		Provide a cardboard box for each student in his bedroom for returned school papers.	

Identify Problem: *Bathroom is always a mess.*

Why is it a problem?	Goal or Ideal Situation	Brainstorm Possibilities	To-Do List
Bathtub isn't cleaned immediately after each bath.	Bathroom will be neat and tidy *most* of the time.	Assign someone to be in charge of the bathroom each day.	1. Establish bathroom as top-priority area, giving it a quick pickup and polish twice a day. The first clean-through will be one of the children's morning chores.
Son leaves toys out after bath.	Each user will clean up after self.	Spend 5 minutes every morning cleaning each bathroom.	
Lid isn't screwed on toothpaste.		Get kids to pick up better.	2. Put plastic bucket under sink for bath toys.
Kids spread toothpaste everywhere.		Finish the second bathroom.	3. Take out all toiletries and medical items not used every day and put them in the linen closet—up high.

Sink isn't scoured regularly.

Too much stuff left out that won't fit under sink.

Dirty clothes, shoes, magazines, books, and papers get wet.

Train kids to scrub tub and sink.

Buy and install drawer to hold hair equipment.

Take out seldom-used items.

Get more towel rods.

Put 2 dirty-clothes hampers in bathroom—one for clothing, one for towels.

Put magazine rack in bathroom.

Each person clean up any water on floor after bath or shower.

4. Install two more towel rods so each person can have a spot for own towel.

5. Enforce rule: one who showers or bathes must leave room tidy. If reminder has to be given, assign "extra service" chore.

PROBLEM SOLVING

Identify Problem: *Mother turns into grizzly bear at 4:00 P.M.*

Why is it a problem?	Goal or Ideal Situation	Brainstorm Possibilities	To-Do List
We are all tired and hungry and I can't think of anything for dinner.	The hours between 4 and 7 will be more of a family time than crisis time.	Go out to eat every night. Decide menus ahead of time.	1. Make dinner decision every day before 10 A.M. and check for necessary ingredients.
I can't remember what we already have in the house that could be cooked.	Mother will not be frustrated about what to feed the hungry crew.	Get necessary ingredients out of freezer or shop at store early in day.	2. Plan menus for at least a week at a time and post them on the refrigerator.
The children are tired and competing for my attention.		Hire preteen to play with children at preparation time.	3. Quit project before kids arrive home from school.
The daily project always takes longer than expected, running into dinnertime.		Finish up projects of the day earlier, allowing ample time for meal preparation.	4. Begin dinner preparations by 4:30.
			5. Keep several quick meals in freezer for emergencies.
			6. Mother take a short nap in the afternoon.
			7. Give children a nutritious snack after school.

Identify Problem: *Business stuff is all over our home; it's like living in the office. Some records are lost.*

Why is it a problem?	Goal or Ideal Situation	Brainstorm Possibilities	To-Do List
For financial reasons, we must continue to keep part of the business at home.	Keep business supplies, records, mail, and books in a specified area so we can "live" in the rest of the house.	Get rid of unneeded stuff.	1. Put folding doors across recreation room to divide room.
Everything is located in a different part of the house.		Give up a bedroom.	2. Set up desk, table, file, and shelves for business supplies and papers.
We are not careful to put everything back where it came from.		Divide the recreation room.	3. Keep all business-related items in one area, completely separating home from business.
		Make a large worktable by laying a door across the top of two small file cabinets.	4. Buy basket for desk in which to keep mail and records to go to office.
		Keep business mail and personal mail in separate places.	5. Evaluate supplies, equipment, and books and get rid of the unnecessary.
		Have separate file cabinets for business and personal papers.	6. Install better electric light above desk and table.
			7. Get extension phone for "office" room.

Identify Problem: *I have trouble getting work done with a toddler around.*

Why is it a problem?	Goal or Ideal Situation	Brainstorm Possibilities	To-Do List
He gets things out faster than I can put them away.	Child will remain safe and feel loved and adult will be able to get some things done, too.	Let him watch TV.	1. Accept reality that there will be many interruptions but keep at one job until it's finished.
He always wants me to play with him.		Import an older child for him to play with.	
He wants to be doing everything I am doing.		Quit fighting it; don't try to do as much.	2. Carefully plan time to be doing easier things while he is most active and save the "adult only" jobs for when he is asleep or someone else is here to help entertain him.
He causes so many interruptions!		Put away breakables, plants, and other dangerous objects for now.	
He won't stay out of my projects.		Fence him in.	3. Schedule time just for him so that he knows and I know that time will be his—perhaps mid-morning and before dinner.
		Put latches on screen doors and cupboards.	
		Find ways to keep him busy.	

Baby-sit other children for him to play with.

Trade play time with a neighbor.

4. Give him the bottom kitchen drawer for his toys to play with while in kitchen.

5. Install child-proof latches on cupboards and doors.

6. Hang plants.

7. Let him help where possible—washing plastic dishes or helping scrub the floor.

8. Invite 5-year-old neighbor child to play with toddler for a couple of hours in the morning.

Identify Problem: *What shall I do with all my back issues of magazines?*

Why is it a problem?	Goal or Ideal Situation	Brainstorm Possibilities	To-Do List
I feel obligated to keep magazines. They contain good information that I may need someday.	The back issues I want to keep will be logically stored for easy selection.	Call fire department to inspect premises so they will force me to get rid of them.	1. Accept that there is no moral obligation to keep a magazine forever.
I haven't yet taken time to go through the old issues to take out the articles I want to keep.	There will not be stacks of unread magazines or periodicals waiting to be tossed out or filed.	Discontinue some subscriptions, since I can't read that many.	2. Begin a file system to keep especially good articles.
I don't have a place for so many magazines.		Keep only one year's worth of back issues.	3. Whole magazines will be filed chronologically in cereal boxes on the bookshelf.
It's very hard for me to throw things out.		Keep only those with good articles (that's most of them).	4. I will file or get rid of the last issue the very day the new one arrives.
		Throw out last issue when new one arrives.	5. I will read for 15 minutes every night before going to sleep.
		Find a place to keep old issues.	6. When a new magazine comes, ask:
		Set aside a specific time and day to read.	a. Have I finished the last one?
			b. Have I been reading regularly?

*20
How Well Are Things Going? A Ten-Minute Self-Evaluation

Now that you have learned the basic principles of home management and problem solving and are applying many of them, you are well on your way to having control of your home. But if you do everything I've explained in this book, you have missed the whole idea. I want you to do things for a reason—a reason that fits you and your circumstances, not because it fits at my house. Think about *why* you do things and how you can make your life easier or better.

Now that you have command of the physical aspects of your home, you are freer to live and build to your fullest potential. Winston Churchill once said, "We shape our houses, then our houses shape us." Once you have improved your home environment, other aspects of your life should also improve. Don't expect everything to go perfectly all the time. Even the Yankees don't win every game. You don't want unwaveringly obedient children, a partner who caters to your every whim, or a sterile house. But one of your best rewards from a more organized home is the good feeling you'll have about yourself.

Keep in mind the two most basic home principles: time planning and M M. You can put your house on hold for a long time if necessary just by using those two basics.

CAUTION: As you gain more time and begin to feel on top of things, you may be tempted to take on too many outside obligations and let your home environment slip again. Remember—the reason you sought control was to have more time for yourself and your family—guard that!

HOW WELL AM I DOING?

Review the following evaluation questions two or three times a year to monitor your progress, pinpoint your problems, and highlight your successes. Rate each question from 1 to 5, 5 being the highest possible score.

1. _____ My home is more often straight than messy.
2. _____ My home doesn't rule me; I am in control.
3. _____ I realize I can't do everything, so I choose by planning, not whim.
4. _____ My schedule is flexible.
5. _____ I allow reward time for myself.
6. _____ My schedule is not more important than my family and friends.
7. _____ I use a calendar to record appointments and commitments to avoid overscheduling or forgetting.
8. _____ I take five minutes to plan my daily work, using a To Do List early in my day.
9. _____ I have an established time goal to begin work or projects, before which I have breakfast, pick up and straighten the house.
10. _____ I don't clean deep until the pickup is finished.
11. _____ I use a notebook and keep lists to write in wants, ideas, and things to be done.
12. _____ I operate from a weekly work schedule, trying to plan the best time for each job.
13. _____ I alternate jobs that don't need to be done each day.
14. _____ I bunch work together as much as possible to save time.
15. _____ After a break or interruption, I ask, "What is the best use of my time right now?"
16. _____ I do today's work today. I don't save it up for tomorrow.
17. _____ I avoid interruptions.
18. _____ I don't talk very long on the phone during work time.
19. _____ By setting time limits, I am learning to work quickly.
20. _____ Picking up is a constant habit.
21. _____ I go to work on workdays.
22. _____ I can force myself to do some jobs I really would rather not do.
23. _____ I have a quitting time for cleaning chores.
24. _____ I dress appropriately for the job.
25. _____ I make a place for everything as it comes into the house and try to keep it there.
26. _____ There is an equal balance in our home of what comes in and what goes out.
27. _____ I make a decision of what to do with the mail as it comes in, handling most of it only once.
28. _____ I have a gift shelf with a few birthday, wedding, and general gifts.
29. _____ I put away each article as it is in hand to save coming back to put it away later.

30. _____ I collect good home-management ideas to use in my own home.
31. _____ I go through closets and cupboards at least once a year to clean, straighten, consolidate, and eliminate.
32. _____ The ironing is caught up weekly.
33. _____ After the laundry is finished, all the clean clothes are put away.
34. _____ I hang up only those clothes that are clean, mended, and pressed (ready to wear) in the closet.
35. _____ I accept only usable hand-me-downs, being careful not to accumulate too many.
36. _____ I do not feel obligated to wear out hand-me-downs.
37. _____ The kitchen, entries, and bathrooms are top-priority areas to keep clean.
38. _____ We eat only in designated eating areas.
39. _____ We have a place to store items that are seasonal or not used very often.
40. _____ The kitchen is straightened, with dishes and food put away, after each meal.
41. _____ The kitchen is arranged into work areas: mixing, washing, cooking, and serving.
42. _____ Step-shelves, racks, files, turntables, bins, vertical dividers, and drawer dividers are used to improve our cupboard space.
43. _____ Items that are hazardous are not kept, except in safe places.
44. _____ The car can fit in the garage today!
45. _____ I know what the four basic food groups are and how many servings of each I need daily.
46. _____ I am trying to cut down on sugar, salt, and fats.
47. _____ I am eating more fruit, vegetables, and grain products.
48. _____ I serve a variety of foods, rotating menus.
49. _____ I carefully plan before going grocery shopping, using a budget plan to divide up the food money.
50. _____ I enjoy inviting guests to my home.
51. _____ I recognize the problems in my home and have a program to work on one at a time until I get them under control.
52. _____ I feel good about what I accomplish in my home.

Homes With Children
53. _____ I plan a time for my spouse and my children.
54. _____ My family respects me and my commitments. I am not solely at their beck and call. We work out scheduling conflicts together.
55. _____ I have a definite training program with long- and short-term goals for teaching our children adult skills and work habits for running a home.

56. _____ I delegate fun jobs as well as janitorial jobs.
57. _____ Even though we are training our children, our home is still a refuge from the world, not a sweat shop.
58. _____ When I am teaching a child to work, I define the job, show him or her how to do it, gradually withdraw help, check up, and offer praise.
59. _____ I never redo a child's chore that has passed inspection.
60. _____ I keep my humor while training my apprentice.
61. _____ I try to make work easier for a child by arranging things with the child in mind.
62. _____ I set a time limit for a child to complete his or her responsibilities.
63. _____ I help the children keep their room in order by seeing that they don't have too many clothes, toys, games, books, etc. for the space.
64. _____ Rather than spanking, I use natural or logical consequences if the child decides to test a rule.
65. _____ When a child breaks a rule, I ask him to restate it, so I'm sure he understands it and knows why he is being punished.
66. _____ As a child matures, I adjust rules, change requirements, increase flexibility, and include her in decision making.
67. _____ All medication, detergents, cleaning supplies, and poisonous plants are high enough to be out of little people's reach.

Score Totals:
   230–335: You're doing great; keep up the good work.
   135–230: You have a good start, but keep trying harder.
   Under 135: Read the book again.

Index